Sil Domestic Violence Victims

**Narcissistic Abuse and Invisible Bruises!
Healing from Domestic Abuse,
Recovering from Hidden Abuse, Toxic
Abusive Relationships, Narcissistic
Abuse and Invisible Bruises - Domestic
Violence Survivors Stories**

By

Hadden Robson

Table of Contents

Disclaimer

Even though the author and the publisher worked together to verify that the material contained in this book was accurate at the time of publication.

The author and the publisher shall not be liable to any party for any damage, damage or destruction caused by errors, omissions, inaccuracies, negligence, accident or any other cause.

Introduction

Domestic violence is a situation of abusive, life-threatening attitude that affects individuals, adults, children in all of our cultures irrespective of gender, age, sexual preference, colour, nationality, sexuality, social status, as well as citizenship status.

Opening Credits

The book **SILENT DOMESTIC VIOLENCE VICTIMS**

Narcissistic Abuse and Invisible Bruises! Healing from Domestic Abuse, Recovering from Hidden Abuse, Toxic Abusive Relationships, Narcissistic Abuse and Invisible Bruises - Domestic Violence Survivors Stories

authored by Hadden Robson, one of the authors with best-selling amazon books.

The book explains domestic abuses and various forms which it involves. It also recommends solutions and gives advices, then counselling where necessary.

Copyrights by Hadden Robson 2020

This document aims to provide precise and reliable details on this subject and the problem under discussion.

The product is marketed on the assumption that no officially approved book-keeping or publishing house provides other available funds.

Where a legal or qualified guide is required, a person must have the right to participate in the field.

A statement of principle, which is a subcommittee of the American Bar Association, a committee of publishers and Associations and approved.

The information provided here is correct and reliable, as any lack of attention or other means resulting from the misuse or use of the procedures, procedures or instructions contained therein is the total, and absolute obligation of the user addressed.

The author is not obliged, directly or indirectly, to assume civil or civil liability for any restoration, damage or loss resulting from the data collected here. The respective authors retain all copyrights not kept by the publisher.

The information contained herein is solely and universally available for information purposes. The data is presented without a warranty or promise of any kind.

The trademarks used are without approval, and the patent is issued without the trademark owner's permission or protection.

The logos and labels in this book are the property of the owners themselves and are not associated with this text.

DOMESTIC ABUSE

Home violence can be a disadvantage that the global world is struggling with. It is a situation that powerfully impact people's way of living or operating regardless of their colour, creed, religion, and so on.

Silently, this psychological epidemic has weaved itself into our society's structure.

Since domestic violence varies, we have an inclination to understanding its different types of scenarios which are spread on TV in other to know what it is all about.

We are all too quick in condemning this act, yet guilty of not taking an impactful step in eradicating this predicament in our immediate surrounding; however, we can also dedicate ourselves to the stoppage of this awful crime.

Even now and then, we are predisposed to be trying to find excuses to assist the state to be of everything and justify why we have a propensity.

Monetary abuse is a good example of domestic abuse whereby an abuser takes advantage of their victims financially. It involves improper usage of the victim's money or properties.

The ways and forms of monetary abuse may vary, the abuser may use subtle tactics like manipulation and tricking their victims while some other abusers may resort to bold tactics by being demanding and intimidating their victims.

Non-secular abuse is a type of religious sexual abuse committed by professional educators and clergyman which mainly involves raping and voyeurism. It is a type of abuse which leaves its victims overly devastated emotionally. It also brings about psychological problems like depression, anxiety disorders and PTSD.

The victims of this sexual abuse are often threatened with negative consequences in other to keep their mouth shut by their abuser. The victims also maintain silence due to secrecy, helplessness, entrapment, and the fear of not being taken seriously when revealing abuse: you can imagine the stigma one faces if this happens.

Non-secular abuse can also leave its victims spiritually discouraged when one begins to wonder how people that are supposed to be of good religious act are those who commit this heinous act

Stalking can be a federal offense and has been another way by which abusers make their victims feel cheap.

Majority of ideas people have about domestic abuse is that it is only physical whereas it may differ and some unsuspecting people might not know they are "real victims" until the situations becomes worse

As a result of this, many victims of non-violent home abuse don't think they may be victims.

Generally, children that are brought into violent places and by violent people that show them little affection have the tendency of growing up being violent and with little or no affection. This can also make them potential abusers due to their unethical background.

WHAT IS DOMESTIC VIOLENCE?

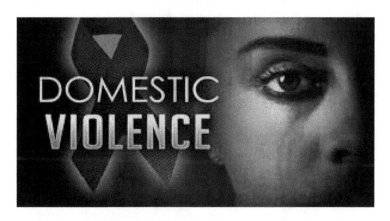

Breaking your silence

Because of the embarrassment, anxiety, abuse, harassment, and trauma suffered, it is always hard to open up about domestic abuse.

Victims believe that the violence will intensify through their abuser directly or indirectly via social media or associates of their abuser. That's why the victims remain silent.

Drop your stigma and let others know if you're a victim of violence. Break your silence if you're a witness to this acts and get support for the victim.

Violence and abuse at home

Many people don't know they're going through violence because they don't know what harassment looks like. Abuse can, however, be much more than physical abuse.

There are different types of control structure in other to curb the power of domestic violence.

Mental/Emotional, Verbal, Financial, sexual, physical, indirect and mental abuse types include.

Psychological Isolation

Involves intimidation and the will to dominate the victim, but is not restricted to only, physical or emotional separation of the victim from friends and relatives, it also involves envy, time control, and distrust of the behaviour of the victim.

The main reason for all this violence is to gain power over the victims and control them.

FINANCIAL

There different types of ways to financially abuse someone:

- Withholding the victims' fund.

- Subtle tricking and manipulation of their victims into giving them money

- Ridiculing their inability to spend correctly, deriding their inability to save.

- Monitoring credit cards.

- Stopping or proscribing access to their account.

- Stealing cash.

- Not letting the victim realize their present-day circle of relative's economic standing.

- Forcing the victim to cash in or sign over belongings.

- Sabotaging employment possibilities.

- Refusing to pay bills.

- Insisting they pay the abusers' payments.

- Hiding check-books or credit paying cards.

Financial abuse is something that gives abuser power and manipulation over their victims in any economic or financial way.

Sexual

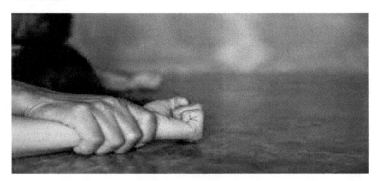

Sexual abuse has been described as anything associated to the sexual intercourse by coercion, which includes but isn't always restricted to rape which hurts the victim emotionally and physically and can add to sexual problems .It can be noted that some victims have had sexual problems after being assaulted sexually.

Physical

Physical abuse is any harm, pain, or impairment and a non-accidental force in nature.

Indirect

An abuser may not usually directly abuse their victims. They may often use different people or objects to abuse their victims. That is referred to as oblique abuse.

At times, perpetrators can use kids to spy on their victim or discredit their victims.

Some abuser will also smear the victim to family and friends, make themselves feel better or like the victim, while turning individual family members and friends against the victim as well, so they will think the victim is insane.

Law enforcement can also be used by criminals to victimize.

There's a lot of ways to crack your silence.

If you were once a victim of domestic violence and you don't know who to talk to, you should try all your possible best to get in touch with the following people:

Your home violence centre.

A member of the Church (religious).

A friend of faith.

If you're not a victim, try helping standing up if you see this abuse happening, and also looking out if you think anyone you love could be abused. Also, it's an affirmation of silence if you keep quiet and act as though nothing is happening.

Please bear in mind that violence affects both the victim and their families regardless of the type. A lot of time, majority of people do not notice the victims suffering, but there will be small hints that may be noted by their family and friends.

The victim may not behave like their usual self, for example, frequent anger, change in moods. If you ask them they might say or pretend as if nothing is wrong.

They may sometimes pretend being happy and try to act so, but deep down they are not. This may be a way to discourage other people from asking or because they don't have enough courage to tell their friends and families. As a friend or family it your a duty to inquire if it's all right and ask if you can help when it might seem nothing is going on.

WARNING SIGNS OR SILENCE ABUSE SUFFERERS

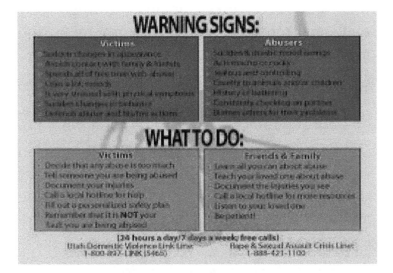

1. You fear your partner's response to a situation more than what it would really be .

I was at a local festival when I was getting back into my friend's vehicle that i noticed that someone had intentionally hit the car's bumper after which the culprit drove away.

I stood there looking at the peeled paint and slightly indented corner, my first reaction turned into frustration of how the situation had turned out to be. Then I started thinking of how my friend will react to this situation and I got even more frustrated thinking about how I could go home and explain to him. I was already thinking if i got home and he saw the state of his car he will start to scream, yell, rant, and rave.I was thinking it wasn't my fault, but to him, it was usually my fault, and all of his anger will become directed at me.

But on getting home when I later explained to him, he only look sober and unhappy and just made it known to me he didn't really like the situation. I apologized and made him reason with me that it could have been him in that same situation and I wouldn't have done anything. The situation went like that and he understood.

In case you spend your days in worry about how your friend is going to react towards you when you offend them or when you make mistakes, then you aren't in a place in which you feel secure together with your friends or even a family member.

If getting stuck at the visitors' and being late to dinner is the lesser trouble than how your accomplice will react to it, you are probably heading toward abuse.

2. It doesn't upset you to argue together with your friend— it scares you.

A fellow female friend of mine once told me that when she argues with the man she's dating, it upsets her. It bothers her that the person she like is either angry at her or that she's irritated with him.

It upsets her due to the fact that she loves him, and she doesn't like having quarrels in their relationship. However, what it doesn't do is scare her.

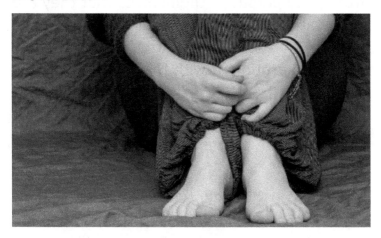

She's not scared that he would possibly hit her in anger. She's not afraid that he's going to run off and cheat on her just because he's irritated at her, or do something else that might be emotionally unfavourable.

Fighting, at the same time as unpleasant as it is, doesn't scare her. If fighting scares you, you would possibly have something to be afraid of.

3. When You Get Right Into A Fight, You Search For The Nearest Way To Go Out.

This can appear self-explanatory, but it's not being followed. Many people don't even consciously understand that they're doing it.

Or even if they do understand it, they often attempt to persuade themselves that they are just irrational because if their partner has in no way hit them before, then why are they always on argument with their partner?

That is your inner intuition telling you that you aren't safe. This is the caution sign that too many human beings pass over and try to ignore.

In case you discover yourself stepping into arguments together with your companion, and in your thoughts, you're already making plans for your getaway, don't brush it off — that little alarm bell can be giving you of a chance that you just haven't seen yet.

4. Don't always accept all what they say is right.

Respect is earned. Many relationships crumble due to the challenges of accepting each other as equal which can sometimes lead to betrayal of trust. But what many people don't understand is that the repeated betrayal of trust is a form of abuse.

Always think for yourself. Don't try to say or do things just to make people agree with you or please, you'll always end up doing wrong things and worse still some people might not appreciate your effort. Be genuine and always try to have your own mind.

If a friend or a partner suggest something and deep down in your mind, you feel it isn't right, then let it known to them. Don't be afraid if you object they aren't going to be pleased or will get angry at you.

If you always accept what they say is right when you have contrary opinion, then you will not be able to think for yourself.

People might also want to manipulate you because they believe you can't reason enough.

5. They make you feel crazy.

Have you ever had a conversation with a person in which they were look for a way to steer you into saying or doing something bad.

Do you already know the way it makes you feel? It's downright annoying.

This is a form of abuse wherein one individual attempts to manipulate the opposite man or woman with the resource of bending or twisting the truth.

It may be really blatant as they're plainly lying to you. For the reason that outsiders can't see the internal problems of your dating, it's up to you to recognize it.

You might begin to feel like you're going loopy, it can be your companion who is making you feel that way on purpose.

6. You feel like you continually need Their Opinion.

Once you make a huge decision, you need to run it past the man or woman you're dating to look at what he/she thinks of your decision. You'll do that due to the fact you value their opinion, and that you respect it.

But at the end of the day, you're going to weigh your feelings along together with theirs, and that you're nevertheless going to do what's helpful and right for you.

But if you feel like you need to get your friend or partner's point of view on everything you are going through, because they will be angry with you if you don't, then something is wrong.

It can be as "easy" as a difficulty or some co-dependency problem, however, if you're basing your life alternatives, profession options, apparel attire, and lifestyle values around what your friend or partner expects from you or maybe demands from you, you're being controlled. And that manipulation may additionally very well develop into abuse.

7. You don't need to be around anybody,

We've all been there: you come across someone, you become deeply in love with him or her, and need to spend a lot of time with that person.

In some situation one person is ready to start going out but the partner doesn't wish to let them do so.

In case your partner feels comfortably alright in your relationship that they could admire and aid help you in having an outing consisting of only them, you're good to move on.

However, if you find yourself slowly reducing off ties in your friends and family, you need to fear that your associate is keeping you apart.

8. You feel responsible — all of the time.

That is a massive overlooked sign for several domestic violence victims, yet it's often the single ultimate telling signal that abuse can be in the future.

In case you're spending the majority of your relationship feeling responsible, you could have a massive problem.

The first tool an abuser often uses is to control your feelings, utilizing, making their victims seem as if everything is their fault. If they're sad, it's the victim's fault. If things aren't going the right way, it's their victim's fault. If they're "settling" for someone much less than what they deserve, it's the victim's fault for not being much better or "desirable enough" for them.

Because if the entire situation is the victim's fault, then it's never the abuser's fault. And the abuser doesn't need to feel as though they're doing anything wrong...like abusing you.

We have been taught for years that if a person hits you, you're being abused. But the problem is that by the time someone sincerely does hit their victim, they would have been abused for so long that they may not be capable of seeing any possible way out.

WHY DO SUFFERERS BLAME THEMSELVES?

It's very common for victims of abuse to blame themselves. Their abuser blames all of the relationship troubles at their victims, and the victim in turns blames themselves.

While a person berates us through mentioning our man or woman defects, we should understand we're not a perfect human being, it is easy to slowly begin taking the blame and letting the abuser absolutely continue this harmful behaviours towards us.

What does it look like when a survivor of abuse blames themselves? They say things like, "I did make mistakes in the relationship" or "I realize I'm now not clean to get together with." those statements are probably correct.

However, we must take a look at the context and environment of the relationship.

Abusers push their victims to behave in different ways due to their own selfish and bad behaviour.

As for the case of youth abuse, toxic and drunk parents push youngsters and teens to an emotional and physical breaking point. For adults, the same goes for bad companions, family individuals, friends, and spiritual leaders.

While a survivor has either of these emotional responses and the whole thing in between, the abuser feels proven in their proceedings in opposition to the sufferer.

The highlight of obligation has shifted, and it lands squarely at the survivor.

Blaming ourselves is an everyday way that I believe all victims have to address sooner or later in their recovery. Telling ourselves how stupid we have been for falling for a bad person doesn't help our healing.

Words are useful, and our internal thoughts will either assist or prevent our recuperation progress.

Motives

The reason victims wouldn't recognize how they feel as a result of what has happened to them in the past is due to the fact they have not experienced something different. If their dad or mum violated them in a few ways as they grew up, and they couldn't consider anything which is different to what took place, then this will be made because of this reason.

And on the part of the individual that does questions it, in some way, they may have come upon something or someone that suggests that how they had been treated was bad. On-time it would have felt personal, and that is due to the fact that the victim would not have had the capability to realize any different.

Trade Point of View

One may additionally have had a member of their family around who treated them differently, and this gave them some other way of looking at themselves.

But if one does not have this and the only treatment they got is that they had been 'awful' or 'worthless' as an instance, then thinking what came about is going to be a lot harder.

A child

To be brought up by those who have been abusive and do not give a reason for his or her behaviour means that one's childhood upbringing wasn't good. Victims may have known that something wasn't right but their inner thought might not be too strong to accept so.

In order times the abused victims tries to persevere and has no other preference than to accept the harsh treatment they are facing. The abused try to cast off all resistance they have against their unjust treatment , and every part of them may be in agreement with how they are being dealt with. This doesn't solves the problem but makes it even more worse.

A Seed

And much like how a seed will grow into a plant or a tree over time, this internal resistance might also begin to become more useful if it becomes part of a person.

This doesn't mean that this may be a straightforward manner, although, as even though one may not like how they feel, it will have become familiar and what one may become used to.

But, if one hangs in there and maintains the situation, they'll progressively start to come across human beings and situations that make them to look at situations in another way.

And these resources will give them new insights into what took place when communicating with that part of them that thought something was still wrong.

ANGER CAN ALSO LEAD TO DOMESTIC VIOLENCE

Humans without issues get angry. We all our have anger limits (anger threshold).Some people continually get angry, while others seldom experience being easily irritated.

Some get very worn-out due to their anger, while others fail to recognize danger at the same time it takes place.

Some professionals propose that the not unusual person gets irritated in a day.

Exceptional anger makes professionals recommend that getting angry fifteen times a day is more likely not unusual. Irrespective of how frequently we revel in our rage, it's far a common and unavoidable emotion.

Anger may have a good or adverse effect. Even as nicely controlled, anger or annoyance has very few terrible fitness on a person's condition. At its initial level, anger is a signal to you that something in your environment is not right.

It rids you of your hobby and makes you take action to do the wrong thing. The way you end up coping with the anger has very critical consequence stirred in your life and welfare.

However. At the same time, as you get angry, your action can also make others to equally get angry too.

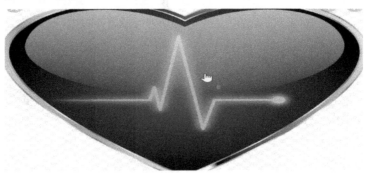

Blood pressures rise, and stress hormones glide. Violence can occur. You may get a reputation as a bad person whom no one wants to relate to due your frequent anger.

Anger alienates friends, co-people, and family. It additionally has a good relationship with health issues and early mortality.

Anger now effectively will increase your danger for an early lack of lifestyles, but additionally, your resort for social isolation, which itself is a first-rate danger element.

Those are, however, some of many reasons why getting to know how to control anger properly is a great concept.

Anger is an ordinary feeling. All people experience irritation every so often.

Different human beings feel and display anger in different ways.

Anger is the number one human emotion; this is normal in everybody, generally caused by an emotional hurt.

Anger is commonly known as an unpleasant feeling that happens while we assume we were injured, mistreated, or while we're faced with limitations that preserve us from conducting our desires.

Anger is "a sturdy feeling of displeasure and feeling of antagonism. It is an unpleasant emotion ranging extensively from infection or annoyance to fury or rage.

The emotion anger, also referred to as wrath or rage, is an immoderate emotional situation. It entails a stiff, uncomfortable, and adversarial response to a perceived provocation, harm.

Someone experiencing anger will often encounter situations, like elevated heart pump, multiplied blood stress, and extended levels of body energy. Some people critically look at anger as an emotion that triggers a part of the combat.

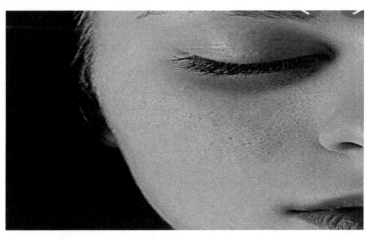

Anger turns into the most critical feeling behaviourally, cognitively, and physiologically while a person makes the conscious desire to do so straight away to prevent the threatening conduct of every other outside pressure.

Out of control, anger can negatively affect personal or social well-being and impact negatively on those around them. At the same time as many philosophers and writers have warned towards the spontaneous and out of control effects of anger which can lead to violence.

The issue of controlling anger has been written about due to the effects the earliest philosophers has cited. But present-day psychologists, in assessment to earlier writers, have also mentioned the possible dangerous effects of not suppressing anger.

Anger is an emotion characterized via antagonism towards to someone or a few aspects you sense has intentionally failed you or treated you incorrectly.

Anger can be a bad component. It can provide you with a behaviour of explicit weak emotions for instance, or inspire you to discover solutions to problems.

But excessive anger can cause problems. Increased blood pressure and one-of-a-kind bodily changes that damage to your physical and intellectual health.

CONTROLLING YOUR ANGER

Therefore, the strength of stopping your anger long-term is not by suppressing it, but by mastering the way to manage and control your anger.

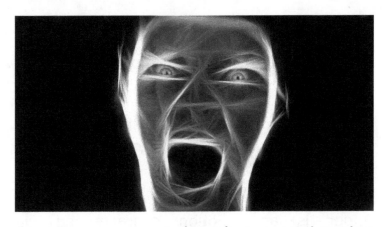

Anger management doesn't suggest ignoring it, which can be as risky as regular explosions. It's about understanding why you're mad and gaining knowledge of how to control your feelings.

Consequently, it is an essential detail of now and then all of us get mad. In reality, from time to time, it's far vital to be angry: as an example, while injustice is done, or while the rights of someone are infringed, it is normal for you to get angry.

Therefore, it's far an essential part of lifestyles.

The way of stopping unnecessary anger is to learn how to control it, just like every other emotion, so that it can be channelled into action.

Anger control skills can help you recognize and talk about what's the reason of your frustration. This may assist you in communicating your message better.

To help us in dealing with strong emotions, many of us have study habits.

Consequently, anger control can be equally learning great extra ways to deal and behave with the problems and frustrations that lead to anger.

Measures towards Controlling Your Anger

There are some steps we will take to help us better manipulate our anger.

Section 1. Starts to understand that rage is just like another emotion, and the first step to being able to manage that emotion is to understand why it happens.

Most of people use anger as a way of covering up their other emotions like tension, weak point, or embarrassment.

That is specifically true for humans who've no longer been allowed as children to express their emotions, but it could differ with another person.

Section 2. We all have certain matters that make us furious, and signs that we are starting to lose our persistence.

In case you lose your mood, studying to understand it could make it less complicated to avoid.

Frequently it is simpler to understand the signs of anger. As an instance, human beings regularly say that after they're indignant, their pulse increases because anger is correlated with the response of adrenaline (combat or fight).

You may additionally discover that for the same motive, your heart is speeding up. You might be anxious and on occasion, clench your fists.

Some people resort to, pacing the ground—again and again, and a response to adrenaline.

Triggers are frequently very unique. However, a ramification of known subjects may additionally assist you to apprehend them.

Terrible forms of the behaviour are often associated with outbursts of anger.

Pay attention in case you begin to over-react ("He by no means supports me!" "She still leaves lying about her shoes!") Or jump to conclusions exactly what people do.

People or situations you find provoking may make your emotions harder and difficult to control. Consequently, if your rage is like a cowl for different emotions, it can show.

Getting mindful of what makes you depressed will help you avoid issues like that, or ask for help to make you control them.

Section three. Learn ways to relax Your temper just as we all have rage causes, so are given methods to' settle down.' Understanding those strategies means that when you find signs your frustration, you could use them to your advantage.

Some beneficial strategies include: Consciously breathing slowly and relaxing and looking for the physical signs and symptoms of frustration is the solution behind this.

Even if you can't cast off for 15 minutes, stopping and taking a few deep breaths (and especially freeing them) will let you relax and come up with time to assume.

Sometimes, just noticing your body's physical changes can help calm you down, because it turns your mind into something other than the current issue.

Slowly counting to 10 (ideally on your head, especially in case you're with others) before you assert or do anything, lets you keep away from doing something which you would possibly regret later.

It'll also help you find the best manner to speak your message.

Stretch yourself, you seem too disturbed while you're disappointed. Slowly working out, you loosen up a little, which reverses a number of the anger's bodily symptoms, making you get calmer once more.

Section 4. Discover different ways to expose Your Anger .While anger is essential, and there are times you need to find a good way to specify your frustration that allows people to hear your message respectfully.

Many ways to ensure this takes place is to control' difficult' conversations. In case you're worried about having a dialogue that would make you feeling disenchanted, then try and take over the scene.

Make notes earlier, flippantly, and assertively outlining what you need to mention during your conversation. At some point in your communication, you are less likely to get facet-tracked if you can consult with your notes.

In case of living on what made you unhappy and frustrated, try to consciously on the way to solve problems, so they do not occur again in the future.

Wait until you chill out from your rage and then express yourself in a calm and amassed manner. Without being competitive, you should be assertive.

Replicate on friendship and do not maintain grudges. We should all understand that everyone is different and that we cannot affect different human beings' emotions, opinions, or actions.

Look at the friendship in preference to dwelling at the immediate issue.

That is extra critical than the 'proper' guy. Try to be realistic and be giving people as they are, no longer as we want them to be. Feeling resentful or grudge towards someone can encourage your frustration and make it tougher to control.

You can't change how different human beings behave or feel. However, you could change how you control situation with others, so pay attention on a superb mind-set.

Use Humour to defuse conditions when angry; it is easy to apply inappropriate sarcasm; introduce some exact humour into probably tough conversations. If you could contain laughter, it will lessen anger and raise the mood.

The simple act of guffawing may go a protracted manner, particularly within the long run, to reduce frustration.

Section 5. Look After yourself if you are well and secure in thoughts and body; any form of emotional control makes less complicated.

And, to put it another way, it is harder to manipulate and master our feelings when we are under pressure— which can be harmful. Therefore, taking steps to make sure which you do things properly well is important.

HOW TO MANAGE MY ANGER

The time and standard of anger management classes differ.

While some stretch over several weeks and start getting the counselling strategy mentioned above, others last only one week.

If you have a promising choice, it's best to choose a more extended class than a shorter one, because longer courses will provide more consistent support for you during the changing process.

Regardless of their duration, you will often be assigned to complete homework assignments by anger management classes and use quizzes to track your progress through the course.

If deciding to enrol in an anger management class, think carefully about your specific needs. In general, do you need help with your frustration, or would you benefit more from a couple-oriented course?

Would a corporate anger management program be more effective if most of the issues arise that in the workplace? Perhaps your boss has asked you or the courts have forced you to attend classes.

In either case, you will need to ensure that you choose an accredited class to keep track of your progress and provide definite proof of your participation and completion.

Self-study can also enhance you to learn different ways to deal with your anger issues on your own.

If you're looking for a more advanced anger management strategy, such as women-specific strategies or corporate executives, your local library or book store may be your best resource.

Today, there are a vast number of books that discuss anger and anger management from a variety of perspectives. At the end of this article, several of these books will be mentioned.

Maybe the best way to learn about your anger issues and understand them is to do some more research.

While the scientific study of anger has gained less attention than other emotional issues, there is strong evidence that some anger management strategies are effective in reducing excessive frustration and developing adaptive coping skills.

Sadly, there is a high standard of anger management services. Some are based on sound scientific research; others have not been subject to analysis and may rely on methods that have not been confirmed or may even be harmful.

The best approaches to handle rage, are based on a cognitive-behavioural system. Briefly, cognitive-behavioural theories tell us that the way we interpret events rather than the events themselves often influence our emotional reactions.

For example, when I get upset because the car is going too slow in front of me, the frustration I feel is more closely tied to my assumptions about how others can drive (i.e., as fast as I want them to) than it is to the situation itself.

Management strategies for cognitive-behavioural anger tend to focus on teaching people how to minimize their emotional and physiological agitation, act in less angry ways, and express their anger in more productive ways. Such programs often stress the development of strategies for self-control.

Many practitioners still use outdated approaches that can cause harm. Programs involving uncontrolled, violent rage speech (e.g., hitting pillows or using foam bats to single objects or shouting in an open area) may provide short-term relief but tend to increase the risk of future issues, including aggressive behaviour.

Just because some anger management techniques have academic support does not mean that all practitioners will skilfully use them. Feeling comfortable with the care provider you choose is crucial.

Anger management is not meant to remove one's feelings of anger or regulate the actions of others. Instead, it aims to help the customer reduce their angry feeling's intensity and frequency and learn to express and easily show their anger in more positive ways.

Treating Anger Disorders: Anger Management Treatment Program Options Uncontrolled anger may affect your relationships, your job, and your health.

Rage can take over your life, leading to depression, violence, and feelings of suicide. Your children, neighbours, and employees may also be at risk from uncontrolled outbursts and erratic behaviours.

If you have problems with anger, you must get the help you need to develop effective management strategies.

There are several services, including inpatient and outpatient care and counselling for mental health. To accommodate a wider variety of patients, executive treatment programs and luxury facilities are also available.

Targeted and successful modern therapies frequently give results in as little as six to eight weeks.

What causes problems associated with anger?

Anger is not a problem in itself. The trouble arises when your rage is uncontrollable, and your conduct is lost.

This lack of reason and rationality can lead to problems of all sorts, including erratic behaviour, aggression, harassment, addictions, and law disorder.

Individuals with anger problems sometimes try to suppress their emotions, thinking that they are unacceptable. This can easily lead to wild emotional outbursts and problems with health.

Is there a rage cure?

Anger isn't something that you can get rid of. It's a natural, safe emotion everywhere felt by all men. Nevertheless, when it gets out of control, rage can become harmful and lead to all kinds of personal issues.

While rage cannot be cured, you can control the strength and impact it has on you. There are practical psychological approaches to control anger and can help you become less reactive.

In the face of people and circumstances you cannot manage, you can even learn to develop more composure.

DOMESTIC VIOLENCE MANAGEMENT STRATEGIES BY SUPPRESSING ANGER

All of us have a reaction to anger, but some strategies can help ensure the excitement does not get out of manage.

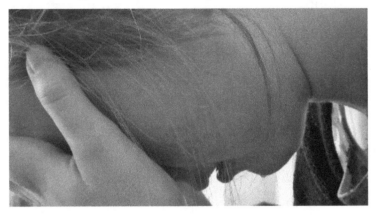

Recognizing the signs of warning. Being aware of changes in the body, feelings, and actions arising from rage will help someone determine how they want to respond before they act.

Pause before you respond. Walking away from the situation will buy some time for the person to reflect and take control back.

The strength of frustration can be decreased by taking a few seconds to count slowly to 10.

Releasing the body's stress. Unlock the neck, lower the shoulders, and uncross the arms and legs to release tension. When retaining tension here, roll back the joints and extend the neck to either side.

Hearing. It can be straightforward and straightforward to reach conclusions when upset. If you have a heated discussion, take some time to stop and listen before you respond.

Learning. Cardiovascular activities like running, cycling, or swimming can help to release the stress that might otherwise turn into aggression.

To find a diversion. Hearing music, dancing, talking, writing in a book, or just taking a shower will help prevent frustration from escalating.

Changing pessimistic ways of thinking. The situation may seem much worse in the heat of the moment than it is. A technique known as cognitive therapy can help challenge people and alleviate angry thoughts.

Use methods of relaxation. Using strategies for recreation, such as deep breathing and progressive muscle relaxation, can help relieve anger feelings.

If anger affects the relationships, employment, and other aspects of a person's life, a doctor may want to seek advice.

Indicators that anger has become an issue include: displaying anger more often than other emotions by harmful or damaging behavioural acts as if rage affects physical or mental health.

Some of the disruptive ways a person can express anger include aggression and violence: this can consist of shouting, swearing and throwing things.

External aggression: This may involve self-harm, self-hatred, not eating, and self-isolation.

Passive aggression: This may include ignoring people, refusing to perform tasks, and being sarcastic, but not saying anything angry or aggressive.

In these cases, seeking support and treatment is necessary. Expressing anger by aggression and violence can be detrimental to friendships, family relationships, and co-worker relationships, and can have serious consequences.

Treatment and counselling from a family doctor can assess and decide whether a person's anger-related problems are related to a physical condition or mental health problem.

If it is a question of mental health, a doctor is most likely to refer the individual to a physician, therapist, or counsellor.

It can help them to make a thorough diagnosis to recommend the best treatment line.

Possible therapies for anger management problems include cognitive-behavioural psychotherapy training for anger management.

Your background and upbringing our upbringing also affects how we learn to cope with angry feelings. Most people receive rage signals as infants that may make it more challenging to handle it as an adult.

For example, you may have grown up believing that violently acting out your anger is always acceptable, so you have not learned how to recognize and handle your angry feelings.

This could mean you've got emotional outbursts when you don't like somebody's behaviours or when you're in a position you don't like.

You might have been raised to believe you shouldn't complain, and you might have been punished as a child for expressing anger.

This may mean you continue to suppress your frustration, and it becomes a long-term problem where you respond inappropriately to new situations with which you are not comfortable.

If you don't feel that you can healthily release your frustration, you can turn it on yourself as well.

When it was out of control, you may have seen the rage of your parents or other adults and learned to think of frustration as something harmful and scary.

This might mean you're scared of your rage now, and you're not feeling safe to express your opinions whenever something makes you unhappy. Then these feelings may occur at another unexpected moment, which may be difficult to explain.

Past experiences if you've encountered specific circumstances in the past that made you feel angry, such as harassment, abuse or harassment (either as a child or more lately as an adult), and you weren't able to express your frustration safely at the time, you may still face those angry feelings right now.

This may mean that you find certain circumstances, especially challenging now, and are more prone to make you angry.

Perhaps the present feeling of rage may not only have to do with the current situation but may also have to do with an experience, which may mean that the frustration you feel in the present is at a level that represents your history.

Being mindful of this can help us find ways to respond more healthily and less anxiously to current circumstances.

Current conditions, if you're going through a lot of other issues in your life right now, you may feel angry more quickly than normal or get upset at unrelated things.

If there is a particular situation that makes you feel angry, but you don't feel you're able to voice your anger directly or address it, then at other times, you might find that you're expressing that frustration.

Anger may be part of the sadness as well. If you have lost an important person close to you, it can be incredibly hard to cope with all the contradictory things you can feel.

Anger's physical consequences trigger the' fight or flight' response of the body. Fear, excitement, and anxiety are other emotions that cause this response.

The adrenal glands are supplying the body with hormones, such as adrenaline and cortisol. In preparation for physical exertion, the brain bumps blood away from the gut and into the muscles.

Blood pressure, heart rate, and breathing are rising, body temperature is growing, and the skin is glowing. The mind is concentrated and sharpened.

ANGER MANAGEMENT TREATMENT FACILITIES.

Residential Anger Management Treatment programs may suggest a housing or inpatient counselling treatment centre if your anger issues seriously affect your daily life.

Exposure to trained care services and monitored facilities may be significant if you find yourself in trouble with the police as a result of anger issues — experience regular, uncontrollable arguments with family members or colleagues.

Physically threatening your kids or other adults threatening violence against others or their properties, your rage and reactive actions can be regulated by a professional.

Residential stress therapies ' advantages help patients learn to control their rage and grievances. The therapist can help you understand dangerous conditions and become more mindful of the warning signs of immediate frustration.

Besides, intense rehabilitation therapies can help you learn how to prevent repression of frustration, which can lead to diabetes, depression, heart problems, and anxiety.

Most significantly, by separating yourself from the outside world's causes and threats, you will build these techniques.

Luxury anger management services Inpatient hospitalization does not have to mean inhuman conditions that are sterile. There are many luxurious services, and they are devoted to professional counselling in the hospital.

Comfortable and serene surroundings have a positive effect on mental wellbeing and mood, and due consideration should be given to treatment facilities.

Executive Counselling Services Corporate counselling programs are available to physicians, managers, attorneys, and other practitioners who, in a separate and private environment, may benefit from one-on-one care.

Successful anger management approaches not only improve individual relationships with employees, patients, and clients but also help provide a framework for sound organizational policies.

Managers and executives should expect to learn how to: identify effective strategies for challenging individuals, experiences and circumstances, Mend broken relationships, regain trust Communication actively reduce emotional reaction with staff and clients, and resolve disputes in a healthy manner.

Anger Recovery and Rehabilitation programs: Sometimes a rehabilitation treatment is dedicated to you if your anger issues aren't physically dangerous and you can't get rid of your everyday life entirely, an outpatient counselling program may be right for you.

Outpatient services include comprehensive individual counselling, usually for six to eight weeks, and help empower patients to move forward with more restricted follow-up treatment.

During your recovery, you're going to have to deal with outside people and situations, so help from friends and family members will make a big difference.

Prescription and over-the-counter medicines since rage is a psychological problem. Medication can be used to treat symptoms.

While the aim of treatment programs should ideally be to make the patient self-sufficient, in the treatment process, different medications may be beneficial.

With anger issues, medications like Prozac, Celera, and Zoloft are commonly prescribed. Such remedies do not combat anger directly within the body, but they do have a calming effect that can help rage management and negative emotion.

Epilepsy medicines are sometimes suggested, mainly if rage reactions arise from a patient's seizures.

You can talk to your doctor if prescription medicines help you with your anger problems. Pay special attention to possible side effects and addiction dangers. Drugs have the function of complementing the recovery, not complicating it.

HOW TO LOCATE THE BEST ANGER DISORDER TREATMENT FACILITY

If you are willing to take care of your anger issues, you need to find help with the question of anger management.

Search for facilities that provide extensive services for diagnosis, recovery, and follow-up. Speak directly to health professionals and ask questions about their skills, methods, and expected outcomes.

Voice any concern you have and ensure that all service expenses are fully understood. In many several cases, at least part of the treatment costs will be covered by health insurance.

TIPS FOR MEDICATION AND RELAPSE.

Unmanaged Rage and Drug Relapse.

Anger may get a little out of control in early recovery. When freshly sober, minor things can cause intense frustration or even explosions.

Sometimes it may seem challenging to learn to be patient without drugs or alcohol. Anger is probably one of the most likely causes of drug relapse. That's why practicing healthy coping skills is so essential to prevent rash decisions in recovery.

Most feelings have been suppressed or hidden with substance abuse among addicts and alcoholics. We switch to a quick fix instead of facing emotion to feel better.

The quick fix is gone once in recovery, and something else has to take its place. It means facing and working through unnecessary and stressful feelings, which I know sounds terrible. Still, it is essential to living a healthy life, maintain meaningful relationships, and prevent drug relapse.

When drugs and alcohol are gone, all the bad feelings come to the surface and may spill over at some point.

Anger is one of an addict or alcoholic's most damaging feelings. Anger has the power to blind a person to act in ways that do not seem logical.

Anger can be built up pressure over time, like any other emotion. Perhaps even months after rehabilitation, inevitably something causes the bottle to explode.

Bottled up rage will cause you or someone else to let it out. Giving up and turning to drugs or alcohol for comfort can be tranquil when in a fit of rage or extreme anger.

When sober, past feelings can also manifest into resentment. An incident that may have triggered grief will turn into anger because, with a sober mind, and you have time to remember the event.

Focusing on a better future or how to forget what happened is crucial not to focus on the past in recovery.

Sometimes making corrections or confronting directly what made you upset can help you move forward. After all, to prevent drug addiction, everything should be done.

Ways to Calm Anger.

As people think of controlling anger, they think of levels in anger management and ways it may be turned off. Although classes can help, it is often unnecessary.

Anger management classes are usually uncontrollable for people with extreme anger issues. Even if that is being said clearly, also, if you don't have a genuine rage problem, you can still be severely damaged by frustration.

Daily activities and healthy coping strategies are essential to rehabilitation for alcoholics and addicts. Anger can be kept to a minimum, and if it is substituted with something positive, opioid relapse can be avoided.

These are some tips to help manage difficult emotions:

Support networks.

They are essential for recovery. Addicts and alcoholics have often spent a great deal of time isolating themselves.

Seclusion lets you change moods without knowing that something is wrong. You can have a group of friends who see you often in a community, or something similar.

You should ask your friends what's wrong if you start to act differently and help you in bad times.

These friends can share their perspectives and help you move beyond what is wrong.

If you feel that you are undergoing too much risk of drug relapse, there may be a support network for you to call for help. You can also help change gears by going to a fellowship meeting.

Meditation / Yoga.

This is crucial to keeping you safe. Not only can meditation relieve frustration, but it is also known to reduce problems with depression, anxiety, and concentration.

Meditation and yoga encourage living and being happy in the present moment, which is essential for calming anger. You might even consider meditation to help you a lot with sleep.

Therapy.

This may make a significant contribution to painful emotions. This helps teach you not to bottle up your feelings, but to get them out and express them.

The source of opioid relapse is bottling feelings. Whether it is for a short period or not, talk therapy can help people understand the value and relaxation from thinking about their feelings.

Walking and exercising.

This is one of the easiest ways to get rid of stress and anger. Even if it's a fast jog or a punching bag with a few punches, physical activity stimulates "feel-good" neurons in the brain.

Working out can help with issues of depression, frustration, anxiety, and concentration.

Hobbies.

Such as art, Having a favorite hobby can not only relieve frustration but can also encourage positive healing and prevent drug relapse.

Among the most important aspects of staying sober is to find love. I find peace in art when I'm angry. I'll be making music, drawing, or painting.

Even if you don't think you're good at something, it doesn't mean you're supposed to try out or make it a regular activity

HIDDEN WOUNDS

After being abused by the individuals who one regarded upon for love and safety, it is going to be a work for a person to completely embrace the reality they should not have been dealt with as they had been.

Deep scars would have been made, so even though time has passed, those will nonetheless define how victims of abuse feels about themselves and lifestyles.

And as infant abuse can be dismissed and denied by way of different human beings, as well as one feeling ashamed of what happened, it can suggest that they don't open up about what passed off.

Validation

One ought to meet someone who treats them otherwise or study exactly something that goes into what they experienced, and their entire world could begin to open up.

Its miles than not just something they have continuously experienced inside them. It's far from something that many others have also long gone through.

They're not going mad, and there is also nothing inherently incorrect with them; they have got without a doubt been doing their best to cope with bad upbringing.

You could then keep in mind that primarily based on what happened, how they feel, and the way they behave is ordinary and to be predicted. And that all people else could grow to be feeling the same if they pass through the same experience.

Attention

Therapists and healers could make this sort of difference, providing they may be aware of this situation.

They can make one to open up about what happened, without one fearing that they are going to be invalidated, overlooked, or close down.

One may additionally have waited a long term to acquire this understanding. But, it does no longer suggest that it's far too long for them to take it.

There will then now not be the need to disclaim how one virtually feels and to keep the emotional loads of their last round with them any further.

Looking at your situation too early in the healing adventure is risky for your restoration.

That would seem counterintuitive, however, any self-reflected early within the process going to be tainted by the abuser's voice, phrases, judgments of you.

In my counselling exercising as a trauma therapist, I have visibly seen this happen time and time again.

My clients know that I push this particular self-reflection verbal exchange away from our early recovery and make it for later times within the recovery system.

I do that, so any false guilt and disgrace from the abuser have already been as it should be addressed.

To recap, patients of mental abuse blame themselves due to the fact their abuser pushed all responsibility onto the victim, and it's clean to tackle lies about ourselves even as it's directed at us with the resource of someone we have relied on.

THE RECOVERY OF EMOTIONAL WOUNDS IS SIMILAR TO BODILY WOUNDS. HOW?

To heal from a physical wound along with a massive cut, you have to begin with the information of knowing where you have an injury.

Then you need to asses if it's far a wound you could control or if its miles an injury which you need help to handle.

Your next step is to smooth out the wound, stitch the wound up if wanted, and in the long run, bandage the wound.

Failure to clean out the wound successfully can cause an infection. Healing from an emotion wound identically works the same way.

Understand you're wounded. Emotional wounds are not as severe as evident as blood pouring from your body; however, they do have a few known signs and symptoms.

They could stem from any range of worrying conditions, which include a death of a loved one, sexual or physical abuse, vehicle accident, divorce, surprising pregnancy, bankruptcy, or problem against the law.

Common signs of emotional wounds are depression, tension, anger outburst, isolation, lacking amusement from existence. Understanding you are wounded and with the aid of what's the primary essential step to take.

Assessing your competencies.

One of the most important steps is to assess if you are capable of controlling the emotional wound yourself or if you need help coping with it.

It's exceedingly essential that you, as it should be decide your abilities as in the example of a large lessen, in case you are incorrect about your ability to manage the wound, the outcomes can be lifelong.

It's extra challenging to clean out an inflamed wound that has already been improperly healed than its miles to deal with it while it is smooth.

When you have presently a traumatic situation, being sincere, in conjunction with your abilities, may be a lifesaving option.

Cleansing your wound.

Well cleaning out a considerable cut cannot always prevent contamination; however, it's going to additionally assist the wound to heal faster than if you left it alone.

Cleansing out the emotional wounds technique involves revising the traumatic occasion and permitting yourself the freedom to experience the emotional ache.

Inside the event of a massive reduction, you may have been coping with a knife improperly; in the fact of an annoying state of affairs, you could now not have understand symptoms and signs of danger.

Stitching your wound.

Sometime, cleaning a massive cut is not enough; you may want a few stitches to facilitate the restoration system and ensure that it heals well.

Stitching up the emotional wounds technique, you understand how other part of your life had been suffering from the trauma.

As an instance, if your companion yells at you ,so you get overly angry and make an outburst—— the wound of verbal abuse wants to be stitched up earlier than facing your companion.

Bandaging your wound.

The final step in the bodily healing of a huge lesson is to bandage it so as keep it from reinjuring the region until it has fully healed.

Emotionally, bandaging up wounds is granting forgiveness, accepting a loss or advantage of existence, being happy with less income, or being peaceful within the midst of a storm.

HEAL FROM EMOTIONAL & VERBAL ABUSE

To admit to ourselves that we've been abused is very significant. Taking action to abusive situations will seem impossible.

And despite the entirety of that, recuperation and rediscovering the reality of oneself will appear not viable as a result of utilizing that time, a person which has been left drained of all energy, desire, and even religion.

1. There is nothing wrong with us.

While getting into a courting, the characteristics of the people we generally tend to love are commonly over appeared. There's no fault for being abused.

The victim moreover must be set free of blame; truly, a negative character hurts people.

To personally take steps to be free and make a best lifestyle for ourselves, we've got significant characteristics of good heart and spirit.

Each person can be a different and exquisite soul as soon as we start to worth and respect that our very own self, and that the skills and trends that we tend to understand blossom the most.

2. Reap Support And Receive The Support With Consideration.

The longer the pain and negative emotions continue to exist in our body system, the further harm they're doing to us.

Having the capacity to speak with trusted family or buddies regarding the situation we have been through can open-up solution, allowing the instinct that radio-controlled us to require action to realize power.

The most challenging part of help is to understand the help that is being presented. Generally, one's believe has been diminished, and having the ability to obtain love, affection, might be tough.

The resources of love and pure friendships are puzzling because it is complicated to get hold of an actual guide while being demeaned.

3. Confirm your worth and Honour Your Self-Esteem.

Take actions that are necessary to reinforce the link and consider you have got your internal self.

Few individuals notice solace in solitude, others in the network. A few people notice dance, art, writing, creativity, work, or specializing in their own family.

What seems easy and straightforward for one man might be tedious and hard for another.

That is that the factor—that is the time to identify and verify for ourselves what works for us and helps our credibleness. Part of maintaining non-public worth is to line substantial obstacles and to live to them.

Putting forward words, once spoken aloud, is healing.

4. Forgive Your Self, Patiently.

Forgiveness is hard, and whereas it is easy to rationalize and recall justification, the feeling of mercy might be elusive. In my knowledge, the hardest man or woman to forgive is one's self.

This unremarkably happens because of agreeing with innocence and intimacy. And to preserve that sensitivity.

Better to recognize your heart and preserve the sacred fact than to finish off completely.

Patience is needed as a result of healing doesn't happens at a time.

5. Laugh a lot.

Laughter makes us brighten, and while getting back from a bad situation.

Being around folks who make you giggle, watching funny films, being around happy folks, will facilitate us change our inner self.

One of my favourite practices is to mention HA, fortissimo, and honestly. And to attempt that again and again, is an exceptionally kind of method in which, it brings real laughter and good sense of humour.

Kind of like starting an automotive engine, the sound may sound empty first of all, but then grows in intensity.

6. Empower our self-possession.

Deep resting, might be a regular a part of restoration from trauma and abuse.

Each day routine, workout, cleanliness, selfless service, and also the culmination of exertions will all be useful for building self-possession and learning to say no, breaking recent behaviour and establishing new styles, all increase self-confidence.

7. Recall devotion and care.

Care is knowing love. And it takes time, persistence, and tenderness with oneself that may not be provided by others.

Only after first seeing and acknowledging the comprehension of oneself can the knowledge we seek from others be conveyed to them.

Free from abusive practices means seeing with honesty what has been done to allow such conduct not to continue.

INCREASE YOUR SELF AFTER EMOTIONAL ABUSE COURTING

Depression, anxiety, and complicated submit-stressful strain disorder are not unusual among survivors of emotional abuse, and the recovery system may be made even greater with the loss of support or outright disbelief in one's self.

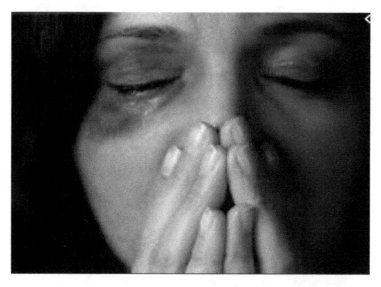

Your intention to stop is right —regardless of how tough humans attempt to take that away from you. You should be heard and to heal.

When an emotionally abusive relationship of any type stops, there is usually a large questions that takes its spot: "Now what?" We decided to create our solution.

We carefully interviewed the survivors of emotional abuse and came up with the following:

1. Take your time.

In an emotionally abusive courting, time is frequently used to tie your interest, affection, and efforts to the abuser. Time 9is strength, and abusers will do the whole lot they could to stop you from having it.

Whether you were not allowed to hang around with a close friend, or you were informed that your lengthy-term vision was a waste of time, or you otherwise always wondered, controlled, and gas lighted on the who, what, while, and in which.

You spent some time being out of that relationship which may often cause extra frightening than freeing.

Your life is your own to live, and you could take as much of time you need to deal with it, on what you need, who you want, and where, while, and the excellent steps you wish to take.

Even as the results of abuse can also impact your ability to behave on these things, there is no time restrict on restoration.

Self-care on your phrases.

That slam poetry organization you've usually wanted to sign up for, purchasing the domestic animal you want as a pet or going after the job you want to do can take a while

2. Re-draw your obstacles.

Barriers are a crucial part of practicing love with yourself and others.

Obstacles let you outline your limits—in which they begin, in which they stop, and the phrases that observe as you interact with the people around you.

 Healthy limitations are established through a steady communication that holds the people involved with responsibility, compassion, and expertise.

3. Forgive yourself.

What the abuser did to you is wrong. You by no means deserved it. The guilt, shame, and fear are not what you deserve now, or ever again.

Out of all of the matters that you deserve, self-forgiveness is in top of the listing.

Abuse in any form is by no means your fault. It doesn't depend on who the person becomes. It doesn't depend on how they got into your life. It doesn't rely on how long the relationship turned out to be. It doesn't matter why you stayed.

None of those subjects however right matters. Here's what does: You made it. You survived. You probably did it.

4. Knowledge is power.

Seeking what to do after, looks as if a hard work on the good days, and entirely not possible on the bad ones.

After however long you have been made to most effectively recognize and understand the world through the abuser's angle, it is sincerely ordinary to revel in confusion—even fear—over in where to start.

Depending on the available resources in your place, there may be applicable workshops, lessons, or seminars you can attend. A short search online can turn up local companies, groups, assist organizations.

If sources are challenging to get right of your entry or you are unable to get in-character guides for any purpose, the internet is your buddy.

5. Take back your story.

People who emotionally abuse others regularly give false stories unto their victims to justify the abuse.

Abusive, fake stories can sound like many of various things. Most of the many types of lies abusers inform their victims is: they're incapable of living their lifestyles without the abuser, that they are 'broken' in some manner, or that no person else will love them.

The abuser is attempting to exchange your truth by altering the way you see yourself.

The conflicting emotions from being informed a fake, harmful tale from a person that you trust or love can be closely damaging, and with long-lasting outcomes.

After an emotionally abusive situation, the lies that the abuser informed you about yourself could continue to have an unfavourable result on the way you view yourself.

While the abuser is thoroughly and securely out of your lifestyles, it's your opportunity to remake your story.

Rebuilding your story is an extraordinarily non-public step, and you don't start things you never have in mind including going public with your tale or sharing it at all.

Irrespective of where you take your story from here, all of the options are yours now.

Emotional abuse and its outcomes are hard to heal. You are reforming yourself from the incidence of months, years, or a long time of damage, and it is very common to feel such as you're struggling because you were severely abused, and that is what abuse does.

Recovery isn't always linear, and the process can take months, years, or a long time. Everyone heals on their very own time.

PHYSICAL ABUSE

Physical abuse may convey immediately damage to a person, but its outcomes can also be long-lasting.

A person who has experienced bodily abuse, mainly in adolescence, may be more likely to enjoy emotional and psychological difficulties later in their life.

Those who've survived domestic violence, abusive dating, or other abuse in maturity might also enjoy pain in connection with the effects of depression long after it had already stopped.

The aid of a therapist or other intellectual fitness professional can often help a man or woman recover from its consequences.

STYLES OF PHYSICAL ABUSE: WHAT CONSTITUTES ABUSE?

Physical abuse can take many forms, and anybody is probably a victim of abuse.

Youngsters are regularly more likely to get abused on the hands of a caretaker, or sibling, at the same time as a grownup might be physically abused by employer, a spouse, companion, or sizeable other.

Elder abuse—mistreatment or forget about an older adult—may consist of bodily abuse and is regularly perpetrated using a caretaker, who is probably a paid professional or a member of the family.

The ones in positions of strength may additionally physically abuse people in their care.

While bodily abuse may be taken into consideration with the aid of a few only to be domestically abused when physical harm is the result, many sorts of behaviours are, in truth, abusive.

It is well known that a person who brings undesirable physical damage to an intimate companion, toddler, or grown-up may be concluded to be abusing that person. These movements can also be described as an attack.

The subsequent actions are commonly taken into consideration to be abusive:

- Punching, kicking, slapping, pinching
- Grabbing or physically restrain in a harmful way.
- Yanking a baby out of the direction of a bicycle is not proceeding to hit the kid and, for that reason, would be considered to be abusing that baby.
- Burning
- Shaking, especially of a baby or small infant
- Beating, whipping.

Some cultures do not accept beating, whipping, or spanking children after misbehaviour to be abusive (some West African cultures). But, this conduct is usually considered to be offensive inside America and in many other nations.

- Poisoning or in any other case causing contamination
- Any shape of planned harm that causes harm

Legal guidelines which includes the Violence against Women Act and the circle of relatives

Violence Prevention and Services Act work to save you and cope with violence in opposition to ladies and children, establish safety and support for victims, provide legal resource and other services to victims of abuse, and offer funding for shelters and packages that deal with home violence on a network level.

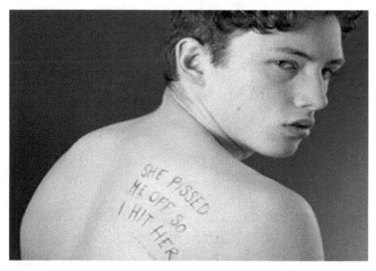

But, legal guidelines defining domestic violence and abuse differ from country to state, and a few states may not offer a lot of protection to victims as compared to others.

In some instances, legal guidelines may offer protection to a survivor of abuse, assault, or home violence.

However, in other cases, help from advocates, help agencies, fitness care professionals, or the police will also be helpful.

The child Abuse Prevention and Treatment Act is an essential piece of legislation that works to maintain all children safe from abuse and damage.

Other laws that works to stop baby abuse consist of mandatory reporting legal guidelines, which require all health care professionals and lots of different those who work intently with youngsters to document infant abuse, whether it is recognized or only somewhat suspected.

Symptoms of Physical Abuse

Physical signs of abuse may include burns and scalds—mainly people who seem mostly or unnatural patterns—bruises, chunk marks, frequent fractures or broken bones, persistent accidents, or continual fitness issues.

But, the presence of any of those bodily signs won't always imply abuse, mainly in kids, who may be vulnerable to falls or other accidents that cause injury.

While a person has frequent accidents or bruises, when the accidents seem to have a sample, or while the explanation of the injury does not seem convincing, then investigation of the scenario can be endorsed.

Individuals—adults and children—who appear all of sudden frustrated, hectic, or who exhibit any of the following behavioural symptoms, in particular with the physical symptoms listed, can be experiencing abuse:

- Insomnia, Nightmares.
- Bedwetting or soiling oneself (in kids)
- the usage of capsules or alcohol
- Self-harming, threatening self-damage
- Suicidal ideation, threatening suicide
- Changes in ingesting behaviour.
- Clingy conduct, a depressive or low mood
- Obsessive behaviour

At the same time, as abuse of small children is usually a critical problem, shaking or throwing a child or small baby can be fatal.

Injuries obtained because of a head injury, while deadly, can also lead to mental damage, disability, speech or a visual impairment, or getting to know problems later in life.

Infants who've been shaken might also maintain internal injuries, broken bones, or fractures. While breathing problems, seizures, vomiting, irritability, and lethargy. No matter the potential motive, a person who has cause to trust a toddler has been shaken or thrown ought to be seeking medical interest immediately.

Psychological Issues Associated With Bodily Abuse

Abuse will have long-lasting effects. A person who was abused early in life may be much more likely to revel in problems, which include melancholy, anxiety, suicidal ideation, and ingesting disorders later in existence.

The ones who've been abused can also experience post-traumatic pressure, use substances to assist them to deal with trauma, have a problem connecting with others.

Individuals may dissociate or be identified with other conditions associated with personal issues. Children can also develop oppositional defiant behaviours or different conduct issues following severe abuse

Due to the fact, perpetrators of abuse are often depended on by way of those that they harm, a person who has been abused may also experience conflicting emotions concerning the violation.

An individual might also nonetheless love the person who is abusing them and find it hard to reconnect this love with the reality of the abuse.

Some people may additionally believe the abuse is their fault, or be satisfied that it is a one-time event, or fear to leave the abusive companion.

Some little kids who are abused violently may have no one to run to, and some victims of domestic abuse stay with abusive partners for a similar motive.

The constant fear of future abuse and for the safety of oneself and one's children can bring tremendous stress and emotional misery on a person.

Frustration and despair can also occur, and some people who have been abused may additionally self-damage to manage or do forget suicide isn't the best way to stop the abuse.

Someone capable putting back thoughts of abuse may fear that an abusive partner or member of the family may be of similar threat finding it tough to maintain a sense of inner peace with the abuser long after the abuse has stopped.

Remembrance of an abuse experienced, which frequently affects an individual firmly while the person attempts to form an intimate relationship or begin a family, may also reason great misery.

Memories of abuse may be intense, and they may interfere with people's ability to manage their lifestyles.

Although some humans who've been abused can be advised to forget about the painful memories and move ahead in their lives, this project is typically not a clean one, and at the same time as burying the memories may additionally serve some reason, it might not be wholesome or beneficial for a few.

It could be best for individuals who've been abused to examine and cope with their real feelings of anger, anxiety, grief, guilt, or anxiety with the help of mental health professionals.

At some certain point during therapy, some individuals can be able to let go of painful reminiscences and revel in some measure of forgiveness for the person that abused them.

However, if the abuse isn't addressed or dealt with, people may go on to enjoy mental distress and difficulty in the course of their life and can be more likely to become abusive themselves.

LEAVING AN ABUSIVE AFFAIR OR COURTING

It is regularly difficult for a person who has been abused to leave. Kids who are abused via parents or other caretakers can also try to record the abuse, but might not be believed without proper evidence.

While they may be believed, or while abuse is mentioned with the aid of an outsider: consisting of an instructor or childcare issuer, a prolonged investigation may additionally stall the manner and might have the impact of worsening the abuse.

For someone to soundly leave an abusive state of affairs, relationship or marriage, all obstacles and protection issues have to be addressed.

Seventy-five percent of homicides related to home violence occur upon separation, so people who wish to leave an abusive situation may regularly want to have a ramification of protection precautions mounted before attempting to depart.

How Therapy Can Help Deal With Outcomes Of Abuse

Survivors of physical abuse can also find therapy to be beneficial.

A mental health expert can assist people in discovering emotions of anger, grief, frustration, and fear and dealing with situations that have developed as a result of abuse, together with depression, anxiety, and different issues.

Help companies for victims of abuse may be useful to some individuals, and play therapy is often prescribed for children who have been abused.

Function play therapy has also been shown to provide benefit, and when PTSD is found in a person who has survived abuse, Eye movement Desensitization and Reprocessing (EMDR) can be endorsed, because it has demonstrated to be effective at treating trauma.

Due to the fact that abuse could have enormous and lasting results, the therapist will typically focus on keeping apart and addressing these, helping the individual in therapy.

Therapy following abuse may help people regain a feeling of protection and understand how to face future problems.

What You Are Planning To Learn Once You Leave Abusive Relationship

A common idea that concerns people moving on from abusive relationship is that will the trauma stays with you for all times.

Though you finish up during a beautiful relationship, you'll still be lost in your previous one, unable to completely jilt in.

In reality, this is often typically merely an indication you haven't moved on.

For some people, calling it quits with an abusive partner might be tough, and it will take some individuals months, or maybe years, to completely recover.

You can be in pain as a result of how your body and emotions has been mal-treated.

However, in time, if you have left this toxic relationship, you will realize that you will get stronger, resilient, and capable of finding somebody who is not planning to discard you for being you.

Here are basic lessons you'll be able to deduce from the traumatic experience and also the strengths you gain from moving on

1. Victimization sympathy

If you've got an excessive amount of compassion for others, it will mean you begin to honour somebody else's story over your own.

If you are doing this all the time, it will result in you providing for others, while you begin to lose taking care of yourself.

We forget that we need to take care of ourselves first and foremost before we will attend to someone else.

So during this sense, after the break-up, individuals begin to use sympathy as a body politic, and think about sympathy as a burden.

Then, at the moment, you realize you ought not to combat everyone else's energy.

2. The longer that passes, you may keep picturing how perturbing the way you were treated was.

You furthermore might understand what you're willing to tolerate and can be higher at realizing and what will not respect you.

"Boundary areas" tell the 'hell no's in our lives, and typically we've got permission to mention 'hell no" to anyone when needed.

Once we tend to point very clear concerning what our boundaries are, and that we stop seeing them as unhealthy things, we tend to get clear concerning what's unacceptable.

From then, I will trust myself to possess the maximum amount of fun as doable, as a result of your communications with yourself.

3. Gain a brand new perspective

In life, we tend to gain different ideas of things during our life experience. Some individuals are going to be influenced a lot by them than others.

Coming out of abusive relationship will offer you a brand new perspective concerning what you may have looked over within the past, whereas you thought you'd met the love of your life.

4. Coping with Troublesome Individuals Gets Easier

Realizing your boundaries in romantic relationships helps you get into different walks of life too.

You will be ready to say, "here's my line, don't cross it" to individuals in your family, friendly relationship cluster, and even at work.

If you cannot specify what you wish a lot of and what you wish less of or nothing of, then you are not planning to build a way of solidity.

Maybe your boss is not a narcissist. However, they are a bit self-loving and held with their own world.

So if you are an over-giver, you are going to grant quite your colleagues - therefore, you will get burned out and exhausted by it.

So once you do all this and you define your boundaries, you may notice you have got plenty of additional energy.

5. You become additional resilient

The thing that doesn't destroy you makes you a stronger person.Being with a harmful and abusive person will cause you to think you're mentally broken over and another time. As a result of they continually move you and keep demanding additional stuffs from you.

The same kind of living can show you how resilient you actually are, and show you the strengths you never knew you had.

For example, "You recognize he/she tried to interrupt you once, and you are not reaching to break once more, or you've become bolder when talking to your abuser. "It's this ability to regain from adversity or severe events.

Once it involves trauma, people believe that you're going be in the problem for the remainder of your life. However, if you regain and recover, you become a stronger version of yourself."

However, once the fog starts to rise, and you see it for what it really was, you fix yourself. Therefore, you are indestructible.

6. The urge to assist others will increase

Once your energy stops being utterly targeted only on your pain and sorrows, you may begin to understand that you aren't alone.

You are not the first person to be taken advantage of, and you will not be the last, as these forms of people hunt down new victims again and again. Whenever you notice this, you may not be able to let it go.

Instead of being unhappy, you will get a better way of life, and wish to unfold your message. You would possibly even be able to stop it from happening to somebody else.

It might be tough to note the signs of an abuser or wrongdoer. This is often as a result of them being able to pretend well enough. Only if you have got understanding can you be able to see through their mask?

By having the gift of the understanding, you'll be able to help others you're thinking that may be in this situation due to the previous knowledge you've got

7. You'll Be Able to Establish the Red Flags

There is a unit variety of red flags that somebody is not a decent person to be around with. It should be one thing obvious, like rude behaviour, however plenty of the time the signs might only be obvious to someone who've experienced it

Looking back and getting understanding of an unhealthy relationship helps you knows the traits the abuser has towards you within the first place.

Maybe they were mysterious and fascinating, and they don't seem a bad person. But if meeting somebody else causes you to feel a similar approach your abuser did at the start, there may be a danger.

That's your body's way of telling you somebody is unhealthy for you. As you become stronger and far wiser, you become distinguish that which is good for you and what's not.

TOXIC RELATIONSHIP

A toxic relationship may be a relationship characterized by behaviours on the part of the harmful partner that can physically damaging to their partner.

Whereas a healthy relationship contributes to our emotional energy, a harmful relationship damages and drains energy.

A healthy relationship involves mutual caring, respect, and compassion, interest in our partner's welfare and growth, a capability to share management and decision-making, in short, a want for each other's happiness.

A healthy relationship may be a safe relationship, a relationship wherever we will be ourselves without concern, and an area wherever we tend to feel happy and secure. An unhealthy relationship, on the opposite hand, isn't a safe place.

An unhealthy relationship is characterized by insecurity, self-concern, dominance, control. We tend to risk our self by staying in such a relationship. To mention a harmful relationship is damaging at best, a real understatement.

Think of it this way: Even smart relationships take sacrifice and work. After all, our husband, our best friends, and even our families aren't perfect (and, interestingly enough, they'll not see us as perfect either).

We've to find out a way to accommodate and adapt to their mistakes, their faults, their moods, etc., even as they have to learn the way to try to do a similar to us. And it's worthwhile.

And then there are toxic relationships. These relationships have changed into one has the potential, if not corrected, to be extraordinarily detrimental to our well-being.

These relationships aren't really hopeless. However, they need substantial and a lot work if they're to be become well.

Kinds of Toxic Relationships

Even an excellent dating may have brief durations of behaviours we should label toxic at the part of one or each partner. Human beings, in any case, are not pleasant.

Some people have had no formal training in how to relate to others. We frequently have to learn as we grow up in life, hoping that our way of regarding others – commonly found out from our parent's pals – is at least reasonably enough.

As referred to above, however, the disorder is the norm in a poisonous courting. The toxic partner engages in controlling and manipulative behaviours on quite plenty daily activities.

Funny thing is, to the outside world, the toxic partner frequently behaves in an exemplary way.

Observe: Any relationship regarding physical violence or abuse is a true definition of extremely toxic and calls for immediate intervention and, with very few exceptions, separation of the two partners.

Even as these relationships aren't necessarily irreparable, I cannot over emphasize the excessive size of how adverse they are.

If you're in this sort of relationship, get help now!

An abusive person behaves the way he or she does basically for one main reason: he or she believes they ought to be in whole control and ought to have all the power in his or her dating.

Power sharing does not arise in any big way in a toxic relationship. And while power struggles are every day in any dating, specifically within the early stages of a marriage, destructive relationships are characterized by way of one partner insisting on being on a pinnacle of factors.

Have in mind, the methods utilized by such a person to control his or her partner in a toxic dating may additionally moreover or won't be without a problem apparent, even to their companion.

With the above in mind, this allows examining a number of the more common forms of dysfunctional behaviours that a toxic partner may additionally use in a courting with a little difference.

Regularly, a toxic man or woman will use several forms of controlling behaviours to gain his or her wish.

Also, on the equal time as the examples under are most normally visible in marriages and devoted relationships, they're capable of arising in figure-toddler interactions or friendships.

1. Belittler

This kind of poisonous individual will continuously belittle you. He or she will make jest of you, basically implying that your thoughts, ideas, or wishes are silly or you don't know what you are doing.

A toxic friend will not hesitate to belittle you in public, in front of your friends or family.

No matter the way that you could have asked them to stop belittling you, he or she will keep this behaviour, once in a while, disguising it by saying, "I'm kidding.

Can't you take a funny story?" The problem is they will not be kidding, and what they're doing is not a shaggy dog story.

Unfortunately, in case you tolerate this bad conduct long enough, you very well may additionally start to agree with them couldn't make perfect choices.

This individual will regularly inform you that you're lucky to have them as a friend, that no man or woman could need you.

His or her purpose is to reduce your self-esteem as little as possible, so you don't undertake their absolute control of the relationship.

2. The "horrific temper" toxic companion

I have people who frequently will tell me they've given up seeking to argue or disagree with their partner due to the fact he/she gets angry or loses his or her mood and they don't often rl have interaction with them in any meaningful ways for days. "Controlling by the use of intimidation" is a traditional behaviour of a toxic partner.

Regularly these people have an unpredictable and "hair-trigger" mood. Their partners don't know what will ship him or her right into a rage.

This consistent want for vigilance and inability to realize what's going to trigger an angry outburst wears on both the "victim's" emotional and physical fitness.

Once more, it is noteworthy that this emotionally abusive partner hardly ever shows this side of his or her self to the outside world. He or she is often seen as a pleasant, easy - going individual who almost every person likes.

As you will assume, if you confront an abusive angry partner about the inappropriateness of their anger, they will nearly continuously blame their mood outburst on you. Come what may it's your fault they yell and scream. This is a characteristic of a toxic associate.

3. The Guilt-Inducer

A poisonous relationship can, on the way arise not only among individuals in a dedicated dating, however additionally among friends or mother and father and their youngsters.

Control in one's relationships, in addition to in a devoted courting, can be achieved through inducing guilt on the "victims" The guilt inducer controls you with the useful resource of making you to feel accountable and guilty any time you do something she or he doesn't like.

Now not occasionally, they will get someone else to supply their experience of "sadness" or "hurt" to you.

A guilt inducer, not most straightforward controls through inducing guilt but additionally may be quick in "putting off" blame in case you emerge as doing what she or he wishes you to do.

For guilt-susceptible individuals, some issue or all and sundry that eliminates guilt may be very best, so the guilt inducer has an instrumental technique of control at their disposal.

By the way, guilt induction is the maximum characteristic shape of manipulation utilized by a poisonous which kind of controls their adult kids.

Regularly, an associate or high-quality different will cover their guilt-inducing control through seemingly helping a selection you're making – going once more to high school.

But will then bring about guilt through subtly reminding you of the way a whole lot the kids skip over you while you're long past or the way you haven't been paying plenty interest to her or him presently, and so on.

As with every toxic behaviour, guilt-inducing is designed to control your conduct so your toxic partner, or buddy receives what he or she wishes.

4. The Over reactor/Deflector

In case you've ever tried to tell a person that you're sad, harmed or angry about something they did and in an instant reversely finds yourself searching for their sadness, hurt, or anger, you're dealing with an over-reactor/deflector.

You find you are self-comforting them whereas you are the one that needs consolation yourself. And, even worse, you receive horrific remarks about yourself for being "so egocentric,"bad and so on.

135

Unnecessarily to say, your initial difficulty, harm, or sadness gets forgotten as you remorsefully deal with your accomplice's emotions.

For example: You try to express your anger or dislike regarding a few problem or event – your partner stays out along together with his/her friends hours longer than they said they might and doesn't even bother to call – and one way or the other your poisonous companion finds a way to make this your fault!

5. The Over-Dependent Partner

Odd because it could appear, one methodology of poisonous management is for your partner to be therefore passive that you just ought to make most decisions for them.

These poisonous controllers need you to create just about each call for them, from wherever to travel to dinner to what automotive to shop for.

And if you make the wrong decision for your partner, they then abuse you for doing so. Their aim is for you to make mistakes so that they can abuse you when you make this decisions

6. The "Independent" (Non-Dependable) poisonous Controller

This individual often disguises his or her harmful dominant behaviour as merely declaring his or her "independence." "I'm not attending to let anyone control me" is their slogan.

This poisonous individual can solely seldom keep his or her commitments. What these people are up to is dominant you by continuing you unsure concerning what they're attending to do.

The non-dependable one can say they'll decide for you. They'll take the children to a motion picture. They'll etcetera etcetera etcetera, on the other hand, they don't do anything.

They typically have a plausible excuse. However, they merely don't keep their commitments. As a result, they control you by creating it next to not possible for you to develop obligations or plans.

What's even a lot more distressing is that this kind of poisonous individual doesn't make you to feel very safe and secure in your relationship.

It's not merely their behaviour that's unpredictable; you're never quite satisfied that they're remarkably showing emotion committed to you, that you just and your relationship with them is a priority in their life. You'll usually end up posing for support from them, support that they love you.

The anxiety you are feeling in such a relationship will, and sometimes will, eat away at your emotional and physical health.

7. The User

Users – particularly at the start of a relationship – usually appear to be helpful, courteous, and pleasant people. And that they'll stay as long as they're obtaining everything they require from you.

What makes the relationship with a user poisonous is the undeniable fact that you may find yourself never having done enough for them.

A user can sometimes do some little thing for you, sometimes one thing that doesn't inconvenience or is not of value to them.

Be warned:

They do not do anything for you for free. If they do you a favor, it's for them to later induce guilt on you. Staying in a relationship with a user is like paying $1,000 for a candy. You aren't obtaining a lot of for your investment

8. The Possessive (Paranoid) poisonous Controller

This type of toxic individual is bad news. Early in your relationship with them, you will appreciate their "jealousy," notably if it isn't too dominant.

And most, however by no means all, possessives can imply that after you're married or in an exceedingly committed relationship, they'll be only excellent.

Don't believe it for an instant.

These poisonous people can become a lot of and a lot of suspicious and dominant as time goes on.

They'll check the odometer in your automotive to make sure you haven't gone somewhere you "shouldn't," they'll interrogate you if you've got to get late at work, they will, in short, make your life miserable.

Over time they'll be wanting to eliminate any substantive relationships you've got with friends and generally even with family.

They do not see themselves in an exceedingly relationship with you; they see themselves as possessing you

A WAY TO LET GO IN AN ABUSIVE RELATIONSHIP

If life works like a storybook, the person we fall in love with might not be the person that breaks us.

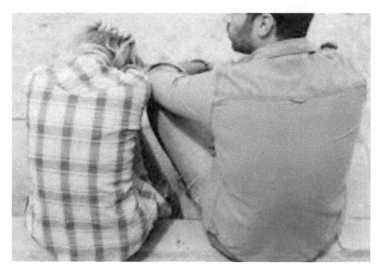

We fall in love, we dedicate, we get damaged– over and over – and we stay.

Humans want human beings, but now and again, the value is a heavy one. While it's a toxic relationship, the breakage can be somewhat damaging.

Love is addictive. So is the choice of love. All relationships may be likened to an addiction, but now and then, the strength of this will be self-adverse.

Even as relationships emerge as tiring, loveless, harmful, stingy, or risky, you'll think they might be easier to depart, but they may be the hardest ones to walk a long way from.

An adverse relationship is one that regularly steals your satisfaction and happiness.On occasion, the symptoms are clear– emotional and physical abuse, consistent grievance, deception, dishonesty, emotional starvation.

Even so often, there is not something outstandingly apparent – it, in reality, doesn't feel right. Perhaps it did once. However, that ended long ago.

The signs and symptoms might also include loneliness, loss of safety, connection or intimacy, or the gap between you every time.

Something it consists of, there are crucial wishes that live hungry, for one in all both humans in the relationship. The connection exists, but that's all it does, and once in a while slightly even that.

Even, some situations are hard to depart, sometimes even though, there's nothing in your way except you.

WHAT TO DO, STAY OR GO.

Leaving any relationship is tough. Going a horrible one isn't usually any less complicated.

The significant changes from powerless to empower is a mild one but lie inside the way you revel in the connection.

It regularly takes as lots of resourcefulness, energy, and electricity to live in a lousy courting because it does to depart.

With a shift in mind set, enjoy and expectation, the sources you use to stay, and to blind worn-out, the seething hopelessness of it all may be used to propel you forward.

Be a gift.

The pull to stay in the future (the way it changed into/ the manner I used to be) or within the future (it'll get higher – I need to find the switch) may be fantastic. However, the energy to move forward exists entirely within the present.

It's always there. However, you want to be in present to access it. To try this, completely experience the connection as it's far, while not having to exchange it or control it.

No relationship is perfect

All couples fight and hurt each others, they say and do things they shouldn't. That's a normal part of the loving and living together.

The problem comes with having to, again and again, live in the past or the future to tolerate – the abuse, the harm, the shortage of self-belief, the jealousy, the loneliness and the grief of the connection because it stands – only so that it's less hard to live.

Keep the rhythm.

Preserve an information of the way you feel inside the dating, the good and bad. If writing isn't your problem, take an image of your face at the same time every day.

You'll see it on your eyes. Snapshots and journaling will capture the intimate, day after day detail of you in this dating. Set a specific period – weeks or months – and at the give up, take a glance over your pox or your writing.

What do you see inside the snapshots? Are you able to understand your lifestyles? Or has it been drained away?

Is that the man or woman you need to be with? Or is it a faded, sadder relationship? This may assist in looking at your relationship for what it truly is.

How do you avoid the truth?

Note what you do to shift far from your reality. Are there risky behaviours you do to stop from feeling awful? Or perhaps there are healthful behaviours that you do in dangerous techniques?

Egocentric.

Ego is ready to recognize what you are and thinking yourself above your true-self. Also making moves to meet those desires.

Be honest on your thing.

Is there something you could do to put the connection back on track? It takes guts to confide in what you may want to do uniquely. However, it's essential.

In case you're now not sure, ask your partner. If only due to the truth your partner names things he or she would love you to do uniquely, it is left for you to decide whether or not that is a right you want to move in.

WHAT'S YOUR ROLE IN THE RELATIONSHIP?

There may be a rhythm within the relationship that keeps it alive. You and your partner can each have a job that follows every other's behaviour attainable. This suggests that over time you'd have fallen into the way of being along that creates a healthy adjustment to an unhealthy state of affairs.

It's usually found in relationships for one person to be the 'reached' and one to be the 'retreater.'

For healthy and secured relationships, this can be balanced, or the roles shift around. There's simple flexibility. In unhealthy relationships, these roles become polarized.

The additional somebody retreats, the further the opposite reaches, and this can be wherever the roles become fastened.

Let go of the fantasy.

The fantasy of what may well be can keep you stuck. Every time. It may well be higher – most higher – however, directly not with this person.

However, does one know? As a result of you've been attempting. And you're tired. And there's nothing additional to offer.

The more you fantasize regarding what may well be, the further truth is embellished and altered into one thing.

The fantasy can persuade you to carry on for a much longer, and perpetually at the value of moving forward, have the illusion that things are going to be completely different.

They won't be. If you have lived the fantasy with this relationship, you'd have done that by now.

Accept what's what.

It's self-contradictory. However, the more you'll settle for wherever you're, the bigger the capability for change. This can let your choices be driven by the info that's real and correct, not a glossed up fairy tale image of what may well be.

Settle for your reality because it is – your relationship, your partner. After you settle for reality, you live the fact.

This can expand your bravery, strength, and capability to choose whether or not this relationship is that the most suitable choice for you – or not. You may have clarity that may propel you forward, no matter what may mean for you.

Fight for "you".

You have to fight for the items you're keen on and also the things you believe, however, one amongst those things has got to be you.

Within you is additional bravery and strength than you may ever need except in some situations.

You're a queen, a king, a fighter, a warrior, you're powerful and exquisite, and everything smart within this world – and you need to be happy.

But first, you may fight for it. Fight for yourself, fight for anyone you're keen on – ferociously, boldly, and bravely.

Stop creating excuses.

Be honest. What do you wish from this relationship? Have you ever had it? However, completely what you want is different from what you have?

How long has it been this way? If you're beloved, it appears like love. Even within the times of a problem, a warm relationship still feels warm.

Despite the strain, the exhaustion, and the things you are doing, or say – a warm relationship provides safety, security, and respect during hard times.

Don't misjudge the reality by claiming to be somewhere in between committing to thing and doing it. You're one or the other.

You're either in it or out of it. Claiming indecision may feel okay within the short term. However, within the future, it'll only keep you stuck while not giving the energy you would need to manoeuvre nearer to what is going to be healthier for you.

If the link feels dangerous, then it's critical for you. That's the sole truth that matters. Fight relentlessly to make your relationship intact. However, once there's no fight left, the reality is going to be staring down on you.

All relationships can undergo make it or break it periods. However, healthy relationships recover. They grow   better and become stronger and more resilient.

Relationships have a restricted amount of resources offered – emotional, physical, and financial. Generally, the connection is going to be disturbed by waves of problem.

If the relationship is healthy, it will solely be a matter of time before it will become flourishing. If it isn't, it'll shrink from lack of nourishment and eventually die.

DOMESTIC VIOLENCE TRAUMA.

A considerable body of studies has documented the connection between abuse and mental health.

Neuroscience have generated new models knowledge for the effect of trauma on survivors of home violence and their children.

These findings offer new insights into the consequences of interpersonal abuse throughout the lifespan, and brings in new techniques for help of the victims.

Intimate partner violence is connected with a wide variety of mental health consequences.

Those who have been identified with substance abuse conditions or who are experiencing psychiatric incapacity are at more risk for abuse, and abusers can also use their partner's intellectual fitness or substance abuse situation to undermine and control them.

CONSEQUENCES OF HOME VIOLENCE ON GIRLS

The results of domestic violence on girl's moves past the immediate physical injuries they go through at the hands of their abusers.

Frequently, home violence survivors are afflicted by series of psychosomatic illnesses, consuming troubles, insomnia, gastrointestinal disturbances, generalized continual pain, and devastating mental health troubles like posttraumatic pressure sickness (PTSD).

Many abused girls find it hard to live their day-to-day lives because of the incident of home violence.

Absences from work, because of accidents or visits to the doctor, frequently cause them to lose their jobs.

They might live in stigma that their partners abuse them, see themselves and not capable of being love, and all other emotional problem.

Because of their emotional situation, some ladies find themselves isolated from friends and circle of relatives and do no longer participate in social activities.

DOMESTIC VIOLENCE AND KIDS

While majority of people listen to or see the phrase 'domestic violence and children,' they see photos of bruised, overwhelmed, burned kids in their thoughts' eye. Sincerely, those physical injuries represent perceived outcomes of domestic abuse.

However, youngsters who only witness domestic violence suffer outcomes just as some of the physically battered youngsters.

Research recommends that children from violent homes, who witness the abuse of their moms at the hands of their fathers, experience mental fitness issues.

Similar studies indicate children, who each witness their fathers abusing their moms and are themselves beaten, go through profound behavioural and emotional misery.

Youngsters who grow up in violent households might also show many poor behaviours and emotions, collectively with:

- come to be violent themselves in reaction to threats (in school or at home)
- try suicide
- Use capsules and abuse alcohol
- Abuse themselves (i.e., reducing)
- tension and despair
- bad social talents

POINTERS FOR DOMESTIC VIOLENCE SURVIVORS

Domestic violence survivors want to be seeking assistance in handling the effects of domestic abuse, in spite of the fact that they have got rid of their abuser.

Whether or not it's been days or years in that the house violence last occurred, domestic abuse survivors can look to their communities for help:

- contact a neighbour-hood home violence useful resource institution

- Make an appointment with a therapist who makes a specialty of treating domestic violence survivors

- Create a complete domestic violence safety plan with the help of a victim assist expert.

The plan will cover a method for taking yourself (and youngsters, if any) to safety within the path of a violent situation.

Hold in the thoughts of jail alternatives. Home violence is against the law in all the states in America. Your close by home violence counsellor or attorney can offer you with records and counselling you on criminal rights.

Viable HEALINGS FROM Domestic TRAUMA.

Many women who have freed themselves from violent home situation have signs and symptoms of (PTSD) long when they have gained physical and emotional safety.

A ringing phone or a crowded metropolis avenue threatens a potential meeting upon their abuser. People they care for seem a long way far off from them, and topics they used to love offer neither delight nor comfort. Their long, sleepless nights drag on.

Based totally on a clinically established set of techniques known as cognitive trauma remedy (CTT), the bodily sports on this book will assist you in dealing with emotions of guilt, anger, melancholy, anxiety, and stress.

You can find out how to interrupt the bad thought in your mind and a way to update them with right and positive ones.

Later within this application, you may be guided through on how to manage publicity from abusing and discrimination of victims.

This system starts-off and ended with techniques for turning your advice and confident character with all the power you want to create the fulfilling existence you deserve.

RECOGNIZE THE NEGATIVE EFFECT OF TRAUMA ON YOUR DAILY LIFE

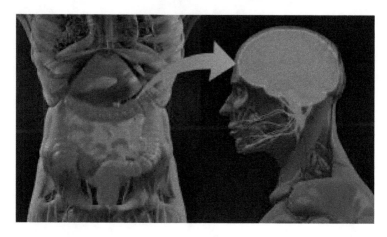

- Let go of frustration, tension, shame, and remorse.

- Avert from core beliefs that result in dysfunctional relationships.

- Confront and overcome your fears.

- Dispel feelings of helplessness.

- Avoid future involvement with potential abusers.

These steps may be accustomed to heal trauma

STEP One: Safety and Stabilization.

Victims of trauma are prone to feel unsafe in their life and relating with others

They'll struggle with controlling their everyday emotions due to the effects of the trauma. It's going to take months or perhaps years to regain a way of safety.

STEP Two: Remembrance And Mourning.

This method is best undertaken with a trained counsellor or healer. It's vital to mourn the losses related to the trauma and provides one area to grieve and specify emotions.

STEP Three: Reconnection and Integration.

Here, survivors acknowledge the impact of the victimization they had, nevertheless begin to believe that trauma isn't any longer a permanent component in their life.

They start to redefine themselves within the context of significant relationships, build a replacement sense of confidence, and build a better future.

In some instances, they'll realize a mission when they heal and grow, like mentoring or changing into an associate advocate for others.

NARCISSISTIC ABUSE

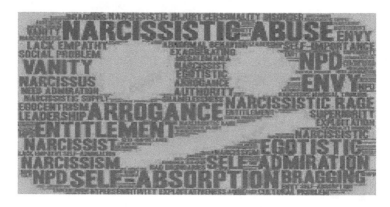

Narcissists don't usually love themselves. They're driven by shame. They try to show the image that they love and admire themselves.

However, deep down narcissists feel the gap between the façade they show the world and their shame-based self. A narcist uses defense mechanisms that are damaging to relationships and cause pain and harm to their beloved ones.

If you're a victim of abuse, the most challenges for you are:

- Clearly distinguishing it;

- Building a support system; and

- Learning the way to strengthen and shield yourself.

- Abuse is also emotional, mental, physical, financial, spiritual, or sexual.

Here are samples of abuse you might not have identified:

Verbal Abuse.

This includes belittling, bullying, accusing, blaming, shaming, demanding, ordering, threatening, criticizing, sarcasm, raging, opposing, undermining, interrupting, blocking, and name-calling.

Note that a lot of folks sometimes build demands, use caustic remark, interrupt, oppose, criticize, blame, or block you. Decide the context, malice, and frequency of the behaviour before labelling it an abuse.

Manipulation.

Generally, manipulation is an indirect influence on somebody to behave in an exceedingly means that furthers the goals of the manipulator. Often, it expresses covert aggression.

Think about a "wolf in sheep's consumer goods." On the surface, the words appear harmless, even complimentary; however, beneath you're feeling demeaned or sense a hostile intent.

Emotional blackmail.

Emotional blackmail might embody threats, anger, warnings, intimidation, or penalty. It's a variety of manipulation that provokes doubt in you. You're feeling worried, obligation, and or guilt,

Gas-lighting.

Intentionally creating distrust in your perceptions of reality or believe that you're mentally incompetent.

Competition.

Competing and one-upping to invariably get on high, typically through unethical suggests that, like cheating in an exceedingly game.

Negative different.

We are unnecessarily creating comparisons to negatively distinct you with the narcist or others.

Sabotage.

Disruptive interference, together with your endeavours or relationships, for the aim of revenge or personal advantage.

Exploitation and objectification.

Using or taking advantage of you for private ends while giving no regard for your feelings or wants.

Lying.

Persistent deception to avoid responsibility or to attain the narcissist's ends.

Withholding.

Withholding such things as cash, sex, communication, information, or fondness from you.

Neglect.

Ignoring the requirements of a baby for whom the offender is accountable. Includes kid endangerment, i.e., putting or leaving a baby in an exceedingly dangerous situation or place.

Privacy invasion.

Ignoring your boundaries by rummaging through your things, phone, mail, denying your physical privacy, or stalking or following you, ignoring privacy you've requested.

Individual Slander.

Spreading malicious gossip or lies about you to different human beings.

Violence consists of blocking off your movement, pulling hair, throwing objects, or destroying your property.

Financial Abuse.

Financial abuse may consists of controlling you through economic domination or draining your budget through extortion, robbery, manipulation, or gambling, or with the aid of the use of accruing debt in your name.

Isolation.

Commonly, narcissists don't take responsibility for his or her conduct and shift the blame to you or others but, some do and are capable of feeling guilt.

A person with more extreme narcissistic trends who behaves in a malicious, hostile manner is taken into consideration to have "malignant narcissism."

Malignant narcissists aren't stricken through guilt. They may be sadistic and take satisfaction in causing ache. They'll be so aggressive and unprincipled that they have interaction in delinquent conduct.

Malignant narcissism can resemble sociopaths. Sociopaths have malformed or broken brains. They display narcissistic dispositions, however now not all narcissists are sociopathic.

Their motivations fluctuate. Whereas narcissists prop up an ideal man or woman to be well-preferred sociopaths alternately to who they will be to obtain their self-serving time table.

They need to win any respect prices which won't be from something of breaking social norms and laws. They don't connect to human beings as narcissists do.

Narcissists don't want to be deserted. They are seriously dependent on others' approval, but sociopaths can without problems walk away from relationships that doesn't serve them.

Even though some narcissists will now and then plot to gain their goals, they are usually extra reactive than sociopaths, who coldly calculate their plans.

OVERCOMING NARCISSIST ABUSE

Even as we're within the midst of an ongoing abuse cycle, it could be hard to pinpoint exactly what we are going through because domestic violence perpetrators can change and turn fact to match their desires.

In case you find yourself experiencing the signs and symptoms under, and you're or had been in a poisonous relationship with an accomplice that disrespects, invalidates and mistreats you.

1. You experience dissociation as a survival mechanism.

You feel emotionally or even bodily different from your environment, experiencing disruptions in your memory, perceptions, and consciousness.

Dissociation can bring about emotional numbing due to terrible situations. Mind-numbing sports, obsessions, addictions, and repression may additionally emerge as a way of life due to the fact of not wanting to face truth.

Your well-known brain shows approaches to emotionally block out the impact of your ache so that you won't be battling with the full terror of your activities.

Those inner elements can embody the internal toddler elements that have been by no means nurtured, the proper anger and disgust you revel towards your abuser might not be visible.

2. You try find off-help.

A not unusual symptom of trauma is fending off whatever that represents reliving the trauma – whether it is people, locations, or activities that pose that threat.

Whether it's your friend, your associate, your members of the family, co-employee, or boss, you discover yourself continuously looking at what you are saying or do around this person lest you

Let them know what's happening to you.

Try and open up to people who can help. Being silent can be deadly and won't help the situation.

But, you find out that this does not work, and you continue to be the abuser's constant target whenever she or he feels like taking you as an emotional punching bag.

You could additionally make more prominent your humans-appealing behaviour outside the abusive relationship, losing your potential to be assertive at the time you are navigating the outside world in particular with people who resemble or are related to your abuser and the abuse.

3. Sacrificing yourself to please the abuser.

You may have been a person who is purpose - oriented and have dreams. Due to abuse, you find yourself living to meet the goals and agenda of a man or woman.

Once the narcissist's life starts to manipulate you, your whole life could start revolving around them.

You could have located your goals, interests, friendships, and private safety at the lowest esteem to make sure that your abuser feels 'glad' in the relationship.

4. Fighting with signs and symptoms that denote the physiological distress

You may have gotten considerable or out of place amount of weight, developed serious fitness troubles that did not exist previously, and experienced bodily symptoms and of untimely getting older.

You find yourself not capable of sleeping or experience terrifying nightmares while you do. Reliving the trauma via emotional or visual flashbacks that bring you again to the world.

5. You are creating a sense of distrust that is universal.

Each individual now poses a severe threat, and you are becoming concerned about other people's intentions, particularly after seeing someone you once trusted in the bad actions. Ultra alert is a reasonable caution.

Since the narcissistic has worked hard to make you think your observations are false, it's hard for you to trust others, even yourself.

6. You have suicidal thoughts or actions that are self-harming.

Growing sense of hopelessness along with anxiety and depression can make you feel that harming yourself is the way out. Even if you wanted to, the conditions feel intolerable as if you couldn't run.

You develop a sense of false consciousness that makes you feel like you don't want another day to happen. As a way to cope, you can even participate in self-harm to yourself.

7. You broaden a pervasive enjoy of distrust.

Absolutely everyone now represents danger and you see your-self becoming stressful about the intentions of others.

Your traditional warning will become hyper-vigilance. So far the narcissistic abuser has worked hard to mislead you into believing that your stories are invalid, you have a hard time trusting all people, which includes yourself.

8. Self-Harming or Suicidal Strive.

As the aspect of despair and tension can also lead to multiplied feelings of hopelessness? Your instances experience unbearable acts as if you can't escape, even in case you favoured to.

9. Isolation

Many abusers isolate their victims, but victims also isolate themselves due to the fact they feel ashamed due to the abuse they're experiencing.

Given the victim blames and misconceptions on emotional and intellectual violence in society. Victims also can be traumatized via law enforcement, family participants, friends, and the harem people of the narcissist who may additionally invalidate their perceptions of the abuse.

They fear no one will understand or side with them, so instead of looking for help, they decide to withdraw from others as a way to keep away from judgment and retaliation from their abuse

10. Comparing Your-Self to Others

Your whole truth has been warped and distorted. You have been mercilessly violated, manipulated, lied to, ridiculed and demeaned.

The man or woman you believe you knew and the life you built together had been shattered into pieces.

Your feel of self- value has been eroded and dwindled. You had been devalued and then shoved away.

In all likelihood, you've been even modified and discarded multiple times, and lured again into an abuse cycle even greater tortures than before.

Maybe you have been relentlessly stalked, burdened, and bullied to stay with your abuser.

But there might not be visible scars to inform the tale, all you have are damaged pieces, fractured reminiscences, and internal war wounds.

11. Worry OF Achieving Something

For the reason that many abusers are engulfed with envy in their victims, they punish them for succeeding. This situations makes their victims to worry about achievement lest they are met with reprisal and reprimand.

As a result, patients are depressed, annoying, lack self-belief and they'll disguise from the highlight and allow their abusers to 'steal' the show time again and again.

SHAMING SURVIVORS.

Home, with its comprehensive explanation of love and protection, isn't always in which you expect to find violence and intimidation.

Home ought not to be an area of pervasive and constant dread, space wherein rape is a reality.

It has to be an area no longer wherein a figure abuse labeling them as lousy, silly, or undoubtedly unworthy of a lifestyle free from such violence.

Disgrace and guilt are also causes of physical violence vulnerable to emerge in a twinkle of an eye.

Such violent acts are continuously discovered with the resource of an insistence that one's moves are tolerable and consequently regular.

It's far a double psychic wound that leaves children feeling rootless and afraid.

Some people have been engulfed by their rage that it's far all outsiders expect from them, while others nevertheless can be not able to agree with and form significant relationships with friends and potential companions.

Children emerge as adults having traumatic testimonies hardly ever contemplated upon if monitored with other kids.

Shame is a form of emotion caused by abuse and violence.

– It's a pity which needs to be displaced from the ones answerable for such suffering to the patients and survivors.

Abusive companions can convince their victims that the abuse is their fault, these companion has manipulated their actions and they make their victims confused and emotionally devastated.

One partner choosing to be abusive is in no way the victim's fault. You probably did not deserve it. There is not anything everybody should ever do without needing to be abused. Both partners deserve to understand themselves at all times.

You don't deserve to be looked down upon or called names, informed who you could or can't be friends with, or to be controlled or damaged.

In a beneficial relationship, every accomplice needs to be able to communicate their feelings without resorting to violence or abuse.

There may be a professional help to be rendered for the survivors, but developing a guide or therapy after experiencing relationship abuse is very critical.

Managing a traumatic experience may be overwhelming, and having someone to speak to about it could be useful.

However, in case you don't feel relaxed talking to buddies or circle of relatives about what you're going through you need to be heard, and your feelings rely on it.

But it's important to remember the fact that you have got the right to pick how you need to live your life.

Self-care is essential. After experiencing something damaging, which includes relationship abuse, self-care may be a large part of recovery.

That might make appearance exclusive for all and sundry. However, some human beings pick journaling, yoga, reading, or merely sleeping. The essential issue is to relieve stress and cope with yourself bodily and mentally.

You could allow yourself to move off the shame

Disgrace is another shape of guilt, and guilt is sincerely in no way compelling. Degradation is some issue that healthy humans tend to feel due to the fact they continually expect they might have done something 'better'.

The reality that you have launched yourself from a load of an abusive relationship and started to construct your existence back again is nothing quick of a miracle.

Maintain telling yourself this, write, dance, paint, draw, and share your enjoyment with the loving relationships now in your life and hold going.

The disgrace will evaporate – it will disappear the closer you take a look at this time for your lifestyles, the higher you take delivery of it, and the extra you honor yourself for going through it and going beyond it.

You Are a Honest Person

This is most likely the most significant reason you thought of leaving wherever you were in the relationship in the first instance.

You're a compassionate, kind, warm one who cares deeply. Few have these attributes and makes you vulnerable.

It puts you in danger if you weren't educated about abuse and violent as a child.

Your worry was real – be comfortable with that.

Human beings do measure programmed with the feeling we tend towards decision which is 'fear'.

These days, there aren't several life and death things we tend to face. However, our worry doesn't understand the real situation.

If your stress levels rise high enough, your natural response is the worry, but still you don't understand that's what you're feeling. Worry unbroken us in this relationship.

The worry of being alone, the fear of being abandoned, the concern of failing (again) the dismay of his reactions, and most significantly, the concern of the shame.

Worry thoughts doesn't care if it's logical. Your anxiety was real, and it takes plenty of support, encouragement, and spirit to stop you from worrying.

A choose to order a shaming sentence for a culprit of intimate partner violence (IPV) could appear rational. Perpetrators unremarkably belittle, humiliate, and disgrace their partners among a more significant pattern of physical abuse.

Survivors usually report feelings of an imperishable sense of shame as a result.

Judicially obligatory reveal that shaming sentences conjointly seem to serve the criminal system's retributive goals, causing a clear public message of intolerance for abusive behaviour.

These sentences might be meant to rehabilitate and assumptive that ethical education flows from public humiliation.

But notwithstanding these stigmatizing sentences have some legitimate purpose whereby any profit is outweighed by the very fact that they undermine the main aim and objectives of violence reduction and survivor safety.

Shaming perpetrators make their victims more vulnerable, not less.

Shame is among the foremost uncomfortable emotions personalities we feel; it usually ends up in profound embarrassment, a way of unhappiness, and a catastrophic loss of dignity.

Acts of aggression violence will give an outlet for restoring one's self-image or gaining back a way of management.

Judicial shaming, contradicts what we tend to perceive concerning making the best conditions for ever-changing behaviour of the perpetrators.

It conjointly ignores what we all know concerning the link between internalized shame and externalized violence: shaming a culprit will increase–not decrease–a survivor's risk of hurt, especially if his partner believes she is somehow liable for the shame obligatory by a 3rd party.

Furthermore, judges ordering public shaming also risk reifying an equivalent behaviour that a culprit is being rebuked, causing confusing messages concerning the acceptableness of shame by the abuse.

The system perpetuates another shaming condition that's itself correlate with IPV: impoverishment.

Routine legal interventions like jail sentences which is obligatory participation in force intervention programs usually cause loss or loss of work or an inability to get employment.

These consequences will preserve or worsen the perpetrators' economic instability. For men whose self-worth might derive apart from their "breadwinner" role, the customarily deeply stigmatizing consequences of financial uncertainty and impoverishment will be enough shaming for them.

Legal interventions meant to curb IPV might once more produce conditions that increase abusive behaviours.

To be sure, efforts to grasp and answer the conditions known as contributory to the employment of violence perpetrators should not be conflated with a disposition to make a case for IPV.

The very fact that a culprit feels shame in spite of however profound that feeling, it doesn't justify his use of violence.

However, we should not tolerate interventions that make a harmful risk of skyrocketing hurt to survivors.

Once IPV happens, both victims and perpetrators need interventions that promote their dignity within the room and on the far side.

In holding perpetrators wrongfully answerable for their abusive behaviour, courts ought to expand on the far side the quality menu of interventions not to pioneer new ways that to wound.

However, to seek out ways to carry perpetrators of IPV responsible whereas conjointly addressing the conditions that contribute to IPV within the 1st place are key important role to be carried out.

CAN THE VICTIM OPT TO DROP VIOLENCE CHARGES?

Let's contemplate a reasonably situation: your spouse has seriously abused you by punching or kicking or choking, and either you or somebody you recognize (family, friends, neighbours, etc.) has contacted the police.

The police arrive and gather proof for a forced charge against your spouse.

The situation is chaotic. You are frightened concerning what would possibly happen. You do not wish to be abused. However, you furthermore might don't want to see your spouse getting into the legal problems.

Several battered spouses have the same feeling but still feel compelled to shield their abusers. You will be wondering whether or not you, should drop charges.

The answer is no. as soon as the prosecutor's has issued a home violence fee, the sufferer has no authority to drop the charges. However, why no more? Home violence is a crime.

Some people believe that victims of crime get troubled by the prices. This is wrong.

Crimes are controlled with the aid of the country, and it is the country that troubles criminal expenses, no longer the victim.

In different times, since you did not solve the problem of the fee, you cannot drop the charge.

In other words, because you did not solve the problem of the charge, you cannot drop the charges against the abuser.

Consequently, it is the nation (and primarily, the prosecutor's office) to determine whether or not to move ahead with the case or drop the domestic violence charges.

Understand that even though you aren't the one to deliver the criminal costs, you will have a crucial function to play as the complaints enhance.

The victim's position in the Case

Victims have many roles to play as a domestic violence case moves forward.

As an example, if there's a trial, then you will probably be required to testify in court against your abuser. However, taken into account that in some states, together with California, you may refuse to testify, though you would possibly pay an excellent fee or be charged with a crime.

You could also be required in the courtroom for some other motives, or to retrieve files or proof for the courtroom. Victims are often added in to give an explanation for their opinions, too.

If the judge is making a decision on whether or not to discharge the abuser, you will be invited to speak about whether you trust the discharge decision and why.

Be conscious that, as a victim, your work does not need to be passive.

In different situations, your role does not have to be restrained to attesting in the criminal case or being invited with the aid of the courtroom to talk about your experience, or retrieving files or proof.

It is entirely within your rights to convey your own civil suit.

As a victim, you can sue your abuser for money to pay in your injuries, salary losses, psychological accidents, or even for the price of living.

You have safety options also. You can try and get a restraining order against your abuser. Restraining rules can assist in providing your safety, especially considering some restraining laws will pressurize your abuser to surrender his or her guns.

If you're afraid of your abuser being released and hurting you again, you must look at this situation so that you can locate a place to live separately.

DIFFERENCE BETWEEN THE CIVIL FIT AND CRIMINAL CASE

In case you're a victim of domestic violence, you may be profoundly contemplating whether or not you want to document a civil in shape against your abuser, although there may be a crook charge already filed.

Consider, crimes are offenses towards the state (best the country can issue or drop costs), and civil attacks are offenses towards sufferers (you may choose to use or not).

There are blessings to submitting a local match. Further to assisting in obtaining money to pay to your injuries, lack of wages, and every other price related to the abuse, a local event is commonly less difficult to win than a crook case.

In a crook case, the abuser needs to be proven responsible "beyond an inexpensive doubt."

The "reasonable doubt" general is usually taken into consideration by about 99 percent. This means the nation would have to prove that there's a 99 percentage hazard that your abuser committed

In a civil case, however, the standard is "preponderance of proof," which is commonly considered a fifty-one percent standard.

This means in a civil case, and you would prove best that it's miles more likely than now not that your abuser dedicated the domestic violence acts.

Changing your statement

Although victims cannot drop domestic violence costs, sufferers often need to exchange or remove their comments from the police and investigators (80-90 percent of home violence sufferers recant).

Recanting is taking lower back your original statement. As an instance, you could have advised police that your spouse changed into beating you, however later need to recant that assertion.

It is commonly now not a great concept to recant except you've got honestly lied to authorities.

Recanting may not always force the state to drop the case for the reason that the state can nonetheless prosecute the fact the usage of police reviews, images, and other evidence.

Also, if you recant, you could face crook charges for falsifying records to law enforcement authorities and the courtroom.

The method following a domestic violence situation can be difficult and emotionally tough. Please touch a local home violence legal professional to help guide you as the manner movements forward.

Are you looking to Drop a home Violence price? Get in touch with a legal professional.

Dropping a home violence price maybe not going, but there can be different things you may do to guard yourself and your youngsters.

In case you want to know more approximately your alternatives while domestic violence expenses are issued, you should touch a local own family regulation attorney today.

CAUSES OF HOME VIOLENCE.

Some human beings with very traditional beliefs may think they have got proper mentality or rights to control the others, and that girls aren't equal to men.

Others may have an undiagnosed character disease or mental disease. Nonetheless, others may additionally have learned this conduct from growing up in a family wherein domestic violence became regular as a normal part of being raised in their family.

A companion's domination may additionally take the form of emotional, bodily, or sexual abuse. Studies propose that violent conduct often is resulting from an interplay of situational and character factors.

That means that abusers study violent conduct from their family, human beings of their community, and different cultural effects as they grow up. They will have seen violence often, or they would have been victims themselves.

A few abusers agreed developing up having been abused as an infant. Children who witness or are the victims of violence might also learn how to accept the same that violence is an affordable manner to resolve quarrel between humans.

Boys who believe that ladies are not to be valued or respectable and who see violence directed against ladies are rather more possible to abuse ladies once they grow old.

Women who witness home violence in their families of the foundation are additional possible to be misused through their husbands.

Although girls are most frequently the sufferer of force, gender roles can be reversed sometimes.

Alcohol and medicines also can contribute to violent behaviour. Someone under the influence of alcohol is probable to direct his or her violent act towards others.

Thus maintaining the intense of drug use to a minimum is also precious for an individual in such situations.

No explanation for force, however, justifies the actions of the offender, nor ought to.

These potential causes are solely to higher understand why offender believes it's acceptable to abuse their partner physically, sexually, psychologically and emotionally.

Offenders must get help for his or her unhealthy and harmful behaviour, or notice themselves living a solitary and lonely life.

Experts don't agree on the underlying causes of force. However, they are do agree that the victim never asks for or causes domestic abuse.

Though most victims of domestic abuse are ladies, men will suffer at the hands of abusive associate partners additionally.

They learned to look at physical and emotional violence as correct ways in which to vent anger and address their internal fears and self-perception problems.

The way they growing up to become so gets bolstered in these ways:

- Victimization Violence And Abuse Techniques Worked To Unravel Issues For Them In The Past.

- They Need To Established Tremendous Control Over Others Through Abuse Techniques.

- Nobody Has Stopped Them Or Reported Them To Authorities

Common triggers that cause's partner abuser:

- Disagreement with their intimate partner.

- Financial problems.

- Desperation once the partner threatens to depart.

- Anger increase.

- Humiliation stemming from issues at work or alternative perceived failures.

- Jealousy and envy.

Many specialists believe psychopathology, developed by growing up in a very violent and abusive house, causes the force to continue.

Witnessing abuse becomes the norm, or being abused, destroys the child's ability to trust others and undermines his or her ability to control emotions.

This produces hostile, dependent, and showing emotion of insecure individuals with a profoundly impaired ability to develop and maintain healthy relationships.

Other specialists believe genetic predisposition plays a part for some. However, only a few studies provide definitive knowledge to support this.

For some, it's their cultures where ancient beliefs place ladies to lower place than men in standing and personal identity.

YOUR PROTECTION CANNOT WAIT IF DIVORCE CAN

In a state of affairs wherein one partner is considering a divorce, those movements are secondary to the immediate safety of a spouse, child, or any family member or friend who's at risk from an abuser.

Many spouses frequently encounter in domestic violence during marriage.

They may be afraid the mere mention of leaving or getting a divorce can intensify the violence, increase outburst and retribution.

It's no longer uncommon for a companion to stay in silence and fear for a long term, untill it is too late.

While home violence happens, your health and safety are in imminent danger. GET OUT right away.

Any mind you have got about getting a divorce can wait. Protecting yourself at all cost is the best thing which you ought to be thinking.

There are protections and techniques in the vicinity to guard you against home violence, but you ought to be silenced by fear or denial.

One of step you may take is to attempt to find a civil order of protection (every so often referred to as a brief restraining order) for you to require your abuser to live far away from you legally.

This could encompass all styles of physical contact, calls, stalking, and restrain the abuser from reaching out to you. Violating this order will bring about the abuser's arrest.

This will provide you with time to consider your options, which involves commencement of divorce proceedings in court.

With the strong assistance of police and social services corporations, you will additionally have time to locate a place without a partner's knowledge of your whereabouts.

You must record a restraining order petition in your county court docket. Many counties provide excellent online information, plus unfastened downloadable forms, so that you may additionally need to commence your search for information at the county court's internet site.

You can additionally go to the court docket clerk's workplace in person to get the office work and ask questions about the technique.

Some courts have self-help facilities with workforce skilled to help you prepare and document your paperwork.

You might be concerned that the courtroom will lament you for not protecting your children from witnessing violence in your home.

But mostly, courts keep in mind that girls who are the victims of domestic abuse often broaden what is once in a while referred to as battered female's syndrome, a condition much like PTSD that makes it challenging to accomplish that.

A short order can later be changed to an everlasting order that can be installed in place for a much more extended period with the same restrictions.

Understand that those orders can be established to any crook charges which might be filed due to suspected physical abuse.

HOW DIVORCE CAN BE TORMENTED BY DOMESTIC ABUSE

In some states where fault-basically based divorce is allowed, domestic violence may be the stated cause you may report for divorce.

Many countries don't have any-fault separation, which means that what a partner needs to do is cite irreconcilable difference as the purpose of a divorce.

If home violence or abuse or marital cruelty can be stated, it may affect the branch of property or provide the victim with an upper hand in agreement. It relies upon the laws in your country.

How Your Child Custody Can Be Laid Low with Home Abuse

Regarding child custody which will be vary to a few degrees from the states, one common thing is that each states consider the exceptional pursuits of a child while making place for the custody in a divorce case.

Usually, most states pick out that each parent has a vital and ongoing part in raising a baby after a divorce, and at the same time.

But, even as domestic violence is found in a marriage and it could be documented, courts can find excessive region regulations on infant custody that will be granted by the authorities and visitation privileges.

Depending on the level/amount of the abuse, which determines privileges, which can be denied ultimately. In other instances, visitation is probably restricted to small home windows of time below the supervision of a courtroom docket-appointed guardian.

After a time frame, it can be viable for an abuser to petition the court docket for more visitation rights. If it can be validated, there was a change through the abuser.

This may be the final court docket ordered which will result into counselling or a few distinctive forms of behaviour change to be filled.

Incorrect accusation of domestic abuse. Way out.

Being falsely accused of domestic violence may come up in a very contentious divorce state of affairs.

Not only can you lose your baby custody or visitation rights. However, you can also face crook prices, and your popularity can be negatively impacted for years yet to come.

Sometimes, so that they can have the upper hand in a custody conflict, a spouse will make this form of false accusation.

If a fake accusation takes place and a restraining order is in place, do not violate it under any circumstances.

What you can do best is to upload credence to the case being made towards you. You can additionally help your case with the useful resource of closing calm in courtroom docket instances.

Bear in mind that if the fee of domestic violence can be confirmed to be false, your accomplice will additionally be the hand in absolutely trouble and will face prices of perjury.

This doesn't happen regularly. Though, considering that police officers are wary of prosecuting ladies for this as it could discourage one of a kind ladies from filing certain instances of home violence.

Dependency treatment

The connection between dependency and domestic violence can form in multiple methods.

One instance of that is while alcoholics and drug addicts create an atmosphere of abuse of their domestic. Another example is the relationship that exists between substance abuse and the trauma associated with experiencing domestic violence.

The suitable remedy will vary depending upon whether or not the patient is a sufferer or offender of domestic violence.

25% of all girls enjoy rape or bodily assault of a few kinds at some stage in their lives.

These girls frequently feel trapped because they are physically intimidated through their abuser or have turn out to be financially dependent on them and cannot cater for themselves or their youngsters by themselves.

Sadly, many of these ladies stay in silence and continue to linger on the abuse issues because of their incapacity to correctly deal with the trauma.

In a number of the most extreme cases, the abuser serves as a provider of medication or alcohol to the sufferer, making more extreme attachment.

Additionally, children who enjoy domestic abuse are at a far more significant hazard for latent drug or alcohol dependency, specifically is that they do not go through trauma treatment.

Remedy FOR ABUSER

While discussing domestic violence, it's important to factor out that present-day abusers are once in a while past victims.

For that reason, they must get treatment to help them deal with their past abuse.

Once they're able to correctly and rationally confront their abusive past, usually through a series of trauma remedies, they are treated for their contemporary anger problems and their substance abuse.

The preliminary affected person evaluation is essential in gaining a genuine and complete understanding of the abuser's records.

Very regularly, disgrace and embarrassment prevent patients from telling the overall tale exactly they were abused.

We offer a non-judgmental ecosystem and attention on addressing an affected individual's dysfunctional past to beautify and give them future hope.

Addiction and home abuse are linked in more approaches than one.

Getting better abusers are taught anger control strategies to help them keep away from relapse, at the same time as victims analyse methods to ease the fear and tension related to their trauma.

Patients will study the coping strategy they find out in-home violence therapy and dependency treatment to preserve their recovery.

Non-secular abuse

There are several methods wherein abuse may be religious abuse. Human beings use different types of meanings, and its very quiet crucial to maintain track of which definition people have in mind.

There may be a feel whereby all abuse can be spiritual abuse. For instance, any shape of infant abuse can harm a toddler's rising spirituality.

The reality that the harm consists of damage to the non-secular self is what makes it non-secular abuse further to whatever different form of abuse is going on.

Some abuse is spiritual abuse as it takes area in a religious vicinity/context. Sexual abuse via a clergyman or pastor, as an example, is undoubtedly a form of religious violence in addition to sexual abuse.

The use of religious truths or biblical texts to harm is another form of spiritual abuse. Now and again, battered victims are instructed that God desires them to be submissive to their husbands.

Once in a while, children who are being molested via their mother and father are counselled that God wishes them to be obedient.

Now and then, people quote, "do not remember yourself more, especially that you ought" to suicidality depressed humans.

Those are examples of spiritual abuse– although what's said is a quote from the Bible, even though 'submission' and 'obedience' are in stylish experience virtues.

Some abuse is spiritual abuse due to the fact the sufferer is seemed to be in a function of non-secular authority.

Coercive spirituality is a shape of non-secular abuse. This is most apparent in totalitarian cults.

But there are many unique kinds of coercion. Compulsive spiritual practices are ideas by some to be suitable sorts of Christian schooling of kids.

A few cases of abuse are religious abuse because it invokes divine authority if you need to manipulate humans into behaviours which meet the desires of the abuser.

DOMESTIC VIOLENCE AWARENESS DAY

The goal of the day is to lift awareness concerning domestic, spousal, and child violence.

Folks wear purple on the day, a colour that has long been employed by ladies seeking justice. Ladies represent the first victims of force. However, both men and ladies are victims.

One in 3 ladies and one in four men have suffered abuse in relationships. The violence experienced by men from ladies is sometimes lower-level violence like slaps, whereas men have a lot of possibilities in extreme violence and can even kill their partners.

With the use of purple nowadays, conversations are started concerning force, with the goal of decreasing it and building healthy relationships.

The elder abuse awareness day

Every year on the Gregorian calendar, month fifteen, World Elder Abuse Awareness Day (WEAAD) is commemorated in America and around the world.

Through WEAAD, we tend to raise awareness concerning the voluminous older adults WHO expertise elder abuse, neglect, and monetary exploitation.

As several as one in ten older Americans get abused or neglected annually, and only a single case out of fourteen cases of elder abuse ever involves the authorities.

How Childhood Abuse Changes the Brain

Studies have said childhood abuse, and neglect ends up in permanent changes to the developing human brain.

These changes in brain structure seem to be vital enough to probably cause psychological and emotional issues in adulthood, like mental disorders and habit.

Researchers used resonance imaging (MRI) technology to spot measured changes in brain structure among young adults who had old childhood abuse or neglect.

There have been evident variations in 9 brain regions between those who had suffered trauma and people who had not.

The most apparent changes were within the brain regions that facilitate balance emotions and impulses, moreover, as egoistic thinking.

The results indicate that folks who went through childhood abuse or neglect treatment have a better risk of having such habit. If they're going down that path as a result of this, they might need a strict time which will be dominant to their urges and creating rational choices because of actual physical changes in their brain development.

Brain Structure

There are several adverse effects of childhood abuse and neglect; however, the brain develops.

A number of these potential effects are:

- A decrease within the size of the hippocampus that is very important in learning and memory.

- A decrease within the size of the nerve tract that functions for feeling, impulses, and arousal, moreover, as an act between the right and left hemisphere hemispheres.

- A decrease within the size of the neural structure, which might affect motor skills and coordination.

- A decrease in the size of the anterior cortex that affects behaviour, equalization, emotions, and perception.

- Too much activity within the corpus amygdaloideum that causes process emotions and severe reactions to probably disagreeable or dangerous things.

- Cortisol levels that square measure either too high or too low that have adverse effects.

- Behavior, Emotions, and function

Because childhood abuse, neglect, and trauma changes brain structure and chemical performance, mistreatment may affect the way children behave, control feeling and performance socially.

The potential effects in the body;

- Feeling scared all the time.

- Being perpetually on alert and unable to relax not withstanding when there is no danger

- A tendency to develop depression or a mental disorder...

- A weakened ability to quickly master regeneration.

- Finding social things more difficult

Other Factors of mistreatment

How childhood abuse or neglect affects an adult depends on how usually the violation occurred; what age the kid was during the abuse; who the maltreated was; whether or not the kid had a dependable, cursive adult in her life as well; how long the abuse lasted; if there have been any interventions within the abuse; the sort and severity of the violation; and alternative individual factors.

WHAT IS FELONY DOMESTIC ABUSE?

A jail conviction have some consequences, along with prison time and having your record permanently scarred with a prison conviction, which also can affect your work to be taken into consideration for lots of housing possibilities and jobs.

However, a misdemeanour conviction is crimes that regularly deliver penalties of as a great deal as 12 months of imprisonment.

The more severe exceptional shape of felony domestic violence is against the law in which one own family or family member commits an excessive act of violence in competition to any other resident of the family.

Domestic violence criminal pointers aren't confined to relationships among spouses, but additionally, consist of violence against different own family individuals.

As an instance, legal domestic violence may arise between people who are dating, between dad and mom and kids, companions, the elderly, and exclusive citizens of the same household.

Similarly, domestic violence also can even arise between people who formerly had a relationship, including an ex-spouse or others who used to stay together.

As mentioned above, home violence jail charges are most usually filed because of assault and violent between spouses. However, domestic prison violence may additionally moreover arise with different sorts of crimes, which include rape, kidnapping, or sexual attack.

What may change a bad conduct into a prison charge?

A home violence charge may also change right into a jail domestic violence rate while there are "stressful elements," that turn smooth attacks into irritated attacks.

Domestic violence incidents are generally categorized as felonies when they involve the following stressful factors;

Acts of violence ensuing in excessive bodily damage to the victim or loss of life.

Bad conduct or acts directed in the direction of minors. Especially very younger kids.

Violent acts or threats that comprise the usage of a deadly weapon (as an instance, threatening the victim with a deadly weapon with the aim of intimidating them).

Bad acts that comprise of sexual abuse, along with rape or sexual attack.

Generally, the prosecutor will examine those mentioned above and various factors even as figuring out whether or not to charge the defendant.

The prosecutor might also additionally evaluate any preceding stated domestic violence incidents of abuse. The prosecutor can also decide on earlier convictions.

WHAT ARE THE PUNISHMENTS FOR FELONY HOME VIOLENCE?

Felony convictions also can often carry similar punishments to domestic violence charge.

But, the results for domestic violence are more intense than that of bad conduct charge of home violence.

Bad conduct domestic violence is punishable via fines or a maximum of three hundred and sixty-five days imprisonment. But, a domestic violence charge fee includes other excessive results, along with:

More substantial penalties, on occasion, numerous thousand of bucks more than a misdemeanour charge.

Incarceration in a nation or federal jail facility, for intervals longer than 12 months.

Moreover, being discovered accountable for home violence results in a loss of many exclusive privileges for the abusers.

A felony home violence charge may additionally result in a loss of gun ownership right, loss of custody or visitation privileges for one's kids, or loss of ability to good housing or employment.

Further, in lots of states, a 3rd home violence charge will convert into a criminal because of previous convictions.

What Protections and remedies are to be had for domestic Violence patients?

In case you are a victim of prison domestic violence abuse, there are various remedies and prison protections to be had for, which include:

Filing a quick Restraining Order (TRO):

Temporary restraining orders are issued by the judge

A TRO can often require the abuser to change residency or keep away from with the victim.

TRO's is generally for brief period until a full investigation can be carried out.

Violation of a brief restraining order to make misconduct home violence charge lead right into a prison;

Permanent Injunction:

A permanent injunction is issued after a complete paying attention and maybe a part of the sentencing for the abuser.

Eternal directives final an indefinite time frame and order the defendant no longer to ever make touch with or come into close to proximity with the victim;

Civil Lawsuit:

In addition to criminal fees, a victim can also additionally file a civil lawsuit to get higher costs together with medical bills or pain and struggling damages.

Custody, toddler, and Spousal manual Order modification.

Other children custody orders may be changed upon a change of home violence.

Criminal domestic violence will commonly bring about the culprit dropping their children custody and visitation rights. Furthermore, child guide orders or spousal manual orders may be issued to protect the injured victims.

Have to I hire a felony professional for my jail Domestic Violence Case?

In case you are a victim of domestic violence, you must immediately look for the assistance of a skilled and knowledgeable lawyer to help you when looking for protections.

An owned family law criminal professional can be vital in helping you file for a brief restraining order or permanent injunction.

In case you are managing domestic violence prison expenses, you want to contact a certified criminal defence professional properly now.

A skilled violent protection lawyer can help you on the situation to hold on your case and stand as an attorney or public defender in front of a court.

Domestic abuse evaluation

A home violence evaluation is used to find out help for lots of humans during the assault around the world that suffer from different forms of domestic violence, mistreatment, or abuse.

Every day charges are filed throughout America of claiming that a domestic partner or accomplice prompted some shape of bodily or mental harm to a family member.

Understanding what to do in case of domestic abuse or mistreatment is essential.

Social employees conduct a diligent interview-based mostly on the reporter's familiarity and understanding of the children and family.

The facts acquired from the six own family functioning regions is then used together with any family or CPS records to decide whether or not the company wishes to intervene or the reporter's task meets the branch's threshold for intervention.

The six (6) family functioning assessment areas are the following:

- What's the size of the maltreatment?

- What are the conditions surrounding any child abuse?

- How do the children function on an everyday basis?

- What are the general parenting practices inside the family?

- What are the disciplinary practices inside the family?

- How do the adults (caregivers) function daily?

The assessments are generally made public to make it clear for involved friends, family individuals, co-personnel, doctors, psychiatrists, and others to determine whether or not a person is no longer the problem of domestic abuse.

You may decide to take a look at to yourself as a self-evaluation for you to decide whether or not or not you've got grounds to file for legal suit toward your home companion.

Educating Social people about this are to be held at community organizations

Take a look at your risk

People are capable of acquiring training in several country run institutions, and any close by police station must have contact statistics for the suitable human beings to get in contact with.

You could get keep of training in a manner to handle home abuse that may are to be had inaccessible if you have been element or knew of a case of domestic abuse.

There are many questions about the check, so one can assist the assessor in determining if you are really facing the difficulty of home abuse or not.

Immediate Actions to take on the results of a domestic Violence evaluation?

The outcomes of those tests should assist the sufferer in being aware of any real dangers to them, and have to tell them how they're able to shield, deal with, and support themselves and their family.

The individual giving the assessment test ought to additionally be capable of providing statistics, resources, and recommend on the manner to move approximately defensive the sufferer.

While the quit goal of the assessment isn't always to reason the sufferers to abandon their abusers or to try and clear up all of the victim's issues, the intention is to offer the assistance that the victim wishes.

This will be being attentive to the problem and giving recommendations on what to do, or it can be providing the touch statistics for appropriate organizations or authorities our bodies to address this hassle.

It could also be getting in touch with a nearby domestic violence felony expert's workplace and managing negotiations among the legal professionals and the victim.

To put together yourself for an evaluation test, it's far crucial that you are inclined to inform the complete truth in a matter.

Honesty is critical if an answer is to be reached.

DOMESTIC VIOLENCE AND CHILDREN

There is a home Violence assessment take a look at created to check juveniles who're showing abusive behaviour at home.

A board of interviewers interviews the juvenile as a way to determine whether or not or no longer is he or she showing abusive conduct.

This conduct includes verbal abuse, substance abuse, or physical abuse to a member of his or her circle of relatives.

Be prepared and recognize the way to address any domestic issues in your private home or place with friends.

WHAT IS SPOUSAL ABUSE?

Spousal abuse is described as a way of domestic violence, it entails one partner controlling their spouse by violence or manipulation.

One companion can be the simplest abuser, or in a few instances, each partner actively abuses every different in a single or extra approach. Spousal abuse may be bodily, sexual, or psychological.

Psychological Outcomes of spousal abuse.

Violent relationships typically undergo a cycle that can be difficult to understand but has mental outcomes on the abused companion.

It regularly begins with tension, arguments, threats, and anger. The one's behaviours and feelings improve inside the relationship and are commonly followed by way of a violent incident that may be physical, emotional, or sexual.

Afterward, the abuser will regularly make attempts to apologize, make excuses, or attempt to reconcile the connection. There may be a period of calm, after which the cycle repeats itself.

This trend of abuse frequently worsens over the years and can lead the victims staying in it for a long period:

- extreme worry
- tension
- melancholy
- Withdrawal from own family, friends, and relationships outdoor the residence
- Posttraumatic strain (PTSD)Suicidal thoughts and tendencies Emotional numbing or detachment
- Inability to sleep well.

How Help Can Assist Spousal Abuse Survivors

The isolation and mental effects of spousal abuse can be triumph over by seeking out the assist an authorized mental health professional who incorporates a counsellor or therapist.

Counselling durations provide patients a secure and private atmosphere to precise their feelings, feelings, and stories.

Looking for the assist of a trauma expert can assist sufferers in coping with any residual anxiety, and therapists also can help with the aid of ways of sharing ways of relieving the strain and pain that may be ongoing.

By searching out for assist, survivors of spousal abuse can look at mechanisms of controlling emotions like anger and worry and begin recovery of the mental wounds left by way of the violation. Institution counselling is any other feasible choice, as connecting with fellow survivors can help in mitigating emotions of isolation.

If you or a cherished one is a sufferer of spousal abuse, please are looking for the assist of a certified mental health expert.

The longer the abuse persists, the extra it may damage the victim physically and psychologically.

Conclusion

Closing Credits

All through the Book

The book **SILENT DOMESTIC VIOLENCE VICTIMS**

Narcissistic Abuse and Invisible Bruises! Healing from Domestic Abuse, Recovering from Hidden Abuse, Toxic Abusive Relationships, Narcissistic Abuse and Invisible Bruises - Domestic Violence Survivors Storiesauthored by Hadden Robson.

After going through the whole book, now you have a full insight on how to handle different domestic abuses and violence. Whether you're a victim or a witness of similar situations.

I hope with this effort, people are enlightened about domestic victims, welfare organisations pay more attention to domestic abuse issues and the whole world is free from domestic violence.

Copyrights by Hadden Robson2020

CPSIA information can be obtained
at www.ICGtesting.com
Printed in the USA
LVHW052311140322
713413LV00013B/1890